THE FAMILY TIE

THE FAMILY TIE

ALLEN FINLEY
✠
LORRY LUTZ

Thomas Nelson Publishers
Nashville • Camden • New York

Revised Edition: Copyright © 1983 by Christian Nationals Evangelism Commission, Inc., 1470 N. 4th St., San Jose, CA 95115-0025.

Original Edition Published by Christian Nationals Press, San Jose, California, 1981.

Published in Nashville, Tennessee, by Thomas Nelson, Inc. and distributed in Canada by Lawson Falle, Ltd., Cambridge, Ontario.

Printed in the United States of America.

Unless otherwise noted, all Scripture references are from the Holy Bible: New International Version. Copyright © 1978 by the New York International Bible Society. Used by permission of Zondervan Bible Publishers.

Scripture quotations marked KJV are from the King James Version of the Bible.

Library of Congress Cataloging in Publication Data

Finley, Allen.
    The Family Tie.

    Bibliography: p.
    1. Indigenous church administration. 2. Missions.
I. Lutz, Lorry. II. Title.
BV2082.I5F56   1983   266'.023'172201724   83-19288
ISBN 0-8407-5859-6

In Christ there is no east or west,
   In Him no south or north;
But one great fellowship of love
   Throughout the whole wide earth.

In Him shall true hearts everywhere
   Their high communion find;
His service is the golden cord
   Close binding all mankind.

Join hands then, brothers of the faith
   Whate'er your race may be;
Who serves my Father as a son
   Is surely kin to me.

John Oxenham

CONTENTS

Foreword—Luis Palau xi
Introduction xiv

1. Paul Chang: A World-Family National 17
2. Have Missions Paid Off? 32
3. What Does the Bible Say about Helping Nationals? .. 44
4. Impressions about National Leaders: True or False? ... 57
5. Assisting Nationals Makes Good Sense 74
6. Let's Face the Problems 90
7. How Did We Get Here from There? 103
8. How to Develop a Relationship with Nationals
   That Works 122
9. What Are the Results of Assisting Nationals? 136
10. Cooperating with Other Missions in Support
    of Nationals 149
11. How We Can Share Our Resources with the Church
    Around the World 158
12. What Our Involvement in National Ministries Can
    Mean to Us 173

Appendix

A. Guidelines for Selection of National Ministries ... 182
B. Principles for Reciprocal Commitment 184

Bibliography 187

FOREWORD

Today, with increasing world tensions and with missionaries being persecuted, murdered, or forced to leave certain countries, I believe we have an obligation, as responsible believers, to show the world the true image of balanced, biblical cooperation between Western and national Christians. We can—and should—demonstrate to a skeptical, scoffing world that the prayer of Jesus Christ in John 17, "so they may be one as we are one," is being answered. We have the privilege of fulfilling in the flesh the expressed desire in that prayer.

Sharing our resources, in the true biblical sense, means coming alongside—holding out a helping hand—sharing encouragement, finances, spiritual counsel and comfort with others.

We need wisdom and foresight to strengthen ties with national Christians, a sensitive spirit to share wisely with them, and compassion to want to work alongside them.

In this exciting and informative book, Allen Finley and Lorry Lutz offer challenging examples of how this can happen. They use Christian Nationals Evangelism Commission as a model. I have been impressed over the years with the wise discretion of their board, and the excellent care they take in providing assistance to national leaders. This demonstrates significant insight and sensitivity, and I thank God for it.

The Apostle Paul spoke of biblical cooperation in Philippians 2 when he said,

If you have any encouragement from being united with Christ, if any comfort from his love, if any fellowship with the Spirit, if any tenderness and compassion, then make my joy complete by being like-minded, having the same love, being one in spirit and purpose. Do nothing out of selfish ambition or vain conceit, but in humility consider others better than yourselves. Each of you should look not only to your own interest, but also to the interest of others (Philippians 2:1–4).

Paul speaks of paying attention to the interest of others. I believe it is our privilege and duty to share our God-given abundance with those in developing nations who feel the burden to fulfill the Great Commission. Unfortunately, many of them find themselves crippled by lack of resources time after time.

We in the affluent West have the privilege of choosing how we will spend our abundance. For most of us there is always money left over after caring for the necessities of life.

In our ministry of crusade evangelism, we have seen thrilling instances of missionary teams and nationals working together for the cause of the gospel of Jesus Christ.

Each campaign begins with an invitation from a united group of evangelical churches. As our team considers and prays, we ask, "Are the members of the body of Christ in this city willing to work together to see thousands of people hear the gospel message of salvation through Jesus Christ? Will they sponsor and support this crusade with all the resources available to them?"

In Latin America, of course, it has been necessary to come alongside with financial support for each crusade. We have tried to supply what was needed—guidance, leadership in crusade evangelism, spiritual training and financial help.

Then we must consider what happens to crusade converts when an evangelistic team leaves a city. Who cares for them, nurtures and disciples them in their Christian walk?

The answer must be: the national church. It is the Christian national in that community—that city—that nation—who must look after the new believers.

As a native-born Argentinian, I believe that the national Christian is the key to winning his nation for Christ. As we inspire, encourage, teach, train, and provide assistance, together we can be used of God to bring the message of salvation to thousands.

I'm delighted that Allen Finley and Lorry Lutz have been able to gather material and put together a book that I know will increase awareness of world evangelism in a marvelous way. Now, as you read *The Family Tie,* may God burden your heart, as He has mine, to do our part in cooperating with the worldwide body of Jesus Christ in biblical evangelism.

Luis Palau
Evangelist

INTRODUCTION

The purpose of this book is to examine the biblical principles and practical applications of sharing resources in the church around the world. These stories are documented by fascinating and generally unknown stories of gifted national leaders so as to be helpful to lay people in the church as well as to missiologists.

In our study of Scripture, we have been impressed at how the early church practiced the ministry of service, fully "supplying the needs of God's people . . ." (2 Cor. 9:12). In context, the Apostle Paul was writing specifically about offerings taken by the churches in Corinth and Macedonia that were to be sent to the Christians in need in other countries and cultures.

That the early Christians felt they were one body (family) is most evident. It is also clear that acting upon that concept, the family shared not only its personnel for preaching and teaching, but also its material possessions for supplying the needs of other members who may have been hurting.

This book will show that while historically the principle of sending personnel has been maintained, the concept of free sharing of resources with other family members in their ministry has not only been neglected, but even resisted and denied. Though there has been hesitancy in past years, today this principle is being rediscovered. There is widespread openness and interest in the subject of assisting nationals.*

Hardly a week passes without our being approached by church and mission leaders asking us to provide documented information on the "how-to's" of supporting national Christians.

The Association of Church Missions Committees (ACMC) has repeatedly scheduled workshops on "Assisting Third World Ministries." Basic material for the workshops was published by the Evangelical Missions Information Service in their *EMISsary* (June, 1980).

At Urbana '79 the idea of supporting a national worker was included in the "Ten Steps of Involvement," offered to young people who returned decision cards—the first time this was ever done. John Kyle, director of missions for Inter-Varsity, encouraged us to put these concepts into book form in time for Urbana '81.

This book also demonstrates how traditional missions have seen their hopes realized by the establishment of strong indigenous churches with unprecedented church growth in many countries of the world. National Christian leaders with proven character, high academic achievement, and intense dedication to Christ are quietly, but surely, moving into the forefront, and there is a steady shift by most leading evangelical missions away from a rigid approach that denies assistance to indigenous ministries.

There is now a great and effective door open to the body of Christ for reaching the world. The Lord Jesus Christ, the Head of His family (the church), has provided the means—both in personnel and resources—to fulfill His mandate.

---

*The term "nationals" in this book refers to citizens of developing nations. We recognize that all people are "nationals" of some country or another. We have used the term, conscious of its varied meanings, but from our proven position of respect for those with whom we serve in ministry.

Now it is up to the "family"—the body—to "edify itself in love," so that the whole body may function as one and complete the task He has given us to do.

We want to thank our secretaries, Martha Barclay and Marilyn Mote, who worked tirelessly to type and retype the manuscript, and Mark Johnson for his creative cover design. We also offer a special word of appreciation for the prayers and encouragement of all the wonderful people at the international headquarters.

Allen Finley
Lorry Lutz
San Jose, California

1
PAUL CHANG:
A WORLD-FAMILY NATIONAL

Chang Bao Hwa, born in China in 1932, is known today by his Western name—Paul Chang. Episodes from his life story dramatize the "family of God working together" concept presented in A FAMILY TIE.

The overnight train to Guilin (formerly Kweilin) pulled out of the Changsha station with a sudden jerk as its great pistons set the giant wheels in motion. Chang Bao Hwa stared out of the dust-streaked window, hardly seeing the city slip by, as its greys and blacks of factories and warehouses blended with the people in their drab Mao jackets. His memories of China had always been in Kodachrome, and the monotony of black and white overwhelmed him. But nothing could suppress the excitement building up inside; the clickity-clack of the accelerating wheels underlined just one incredible thought, *You're going home . . . you're going home . . . you're going home.*

For thirty years, ever since he had fled China as a refugee in 1949, he'd dreamed of this journey—a dream he'd thrust into the back of his mind out of sheer hopelessness.

But now the miraculous had happened. By morning he would be home.

He wasn't sure who would meet him when the train pulled into Guilin station. He'd written his oldest brother that he'd been given a permit to visit China, but there had

17

been no time for a reply. He knew his eighty-one-year-old mother was still alive—though there had been long periods of time during the past thirty years when he'd feared the worst, particularly during the Cultural Revolution in the late sixties when he'd gone for six years without one word from or about his family.

The tiny sleeping compartment was designed for just one passenger. Chang had deliberately chosen these better accommodations so that he would have a good night's sleep before meeting his family. The past few days had been busy, traveling from Hong Kong to Guangzou, where he'd unexpectedly met some Christians who were able to dispose of the Bibles he'd brought with him. After taking a night train to Changsha, he'd spent the next day looking in vain for signs of the Bible school and church he had attended there many years ago. Now he must try to sleep.

Turning off the light, Paul (Chang Bao Hwa's Western name) pulled his heavy coat over his head and settled down on the hard berth. But sleep wouldn't come; it seemed as though the wheels screamed louder . . . *You're going home . . . you're going home . . . you're going home.*

And then in the darkness the memories began crowding in—memories he'd deliberately put out of his mind for so many years:

The snow sparkled under a winter moon as Bao Hwa and his older brother neared the roadblock. He shivered in the penetrating cold; soldiers barricaded the road, their rifles pointing at them; his stomach knotted with fear.

His father had sent him and his brother away, concerned that the approaching confrontation between communists and nationalists would embroil his sons. Many young men were being forced to join one side or the other, and Pastor Chang had no intention of losing his sons in a senseless civil war.

As they'd stood in the front hall ready to leave, Bao Hwa's mother wept and held him close. He was only thirteen and to her mother's heart far too young to be wandering as a refugee, seeking shelter and food wherever he could find it. But Pastor Chang remonstrated, "We're putting Bao Hwa in God's good care, Mother. After all, we have many friends between here and Nanking who will take the boys in and feed them. And when they get to Nanking, they'll be safe with Bao-Yin (older sister)." Bao Hwa hugged his mother, not daring to show the excitement he was feeling.

But now, facing the guns of hostile soldiers, the adventure had turned sour, and he wished himself back home. Before he could blurt out the story they'd rehearsed for such an event, his older brother spoke up, "We're students going back home for the holidays. We have to walk, for we have no money for trains. We're not armed; see, all we have are a few clothes," and he held out the worn satchel in which his mother had stuffed a blanket, a few clothes and a little food, for them to see that he spoke the truth.

Still holding the boys at gunpoint, the men conferred with each other in subdued tones. Then, evidently satisfied that these slender youths with their frightened eyes were no threat, they waved them through the roadblock.

The tension drove all thoughts of cold or hunger from their minds as they hurried along the road in the darkness, heading for a village where their father said they would be sure to find refuge for the night.

The memories of that endless journey were a blur in Paul's mind now. It had taken days to reach Nanking, hiding away in the homes of Christians who had known and loved their father as a kind and good man. Pastor Chang had gone up and down this area preaching and teaching, and even non-Christians respected him. Only once were their lives threatened, when they crossed a lake in an open rowboat, with bullets hitting the water all around them from a communist patrol that had spotted them in restricted territory.

Nanking was another kind of memory—in warm colors—of family, friends, music, visitors and a growing personal relationship with his heavenly Father.

A year after Paul and his brother reached the nationalist capital, his parents were able to move south, and the family was reunited. What an exciting time to be alive! Young people were turning to Christ by the hundreds, for the years of war had exposed a great emptiness in their hearts. The newly formed Chinese Inter-Varsity Fellowship was instrumental in bringing about a great student revival—a totally new development in the church in China. Paul himself responded to the gospel and thrived under the teaching and enthusiasm of young Christians around him.

Paul's father pastored a large church in Nanking, where many of the university students attended. The need for training these young people led to the opening of the Tai-Tung Seminary in 1946 with fifty students. Pastor Chang was asked by the leaders of the China Native Evangelistic Crusade to become its first principal.

The Crusade had thirteen evangelistic bands traveling in the interior provinces of China, and reports of conversions in places where no Christian had ever penetrated before were thrilling. Students of the Tai-Tung Seminary also formed such bands during the school holidays, taking their trumpets and accordians to attract crowds in the villages.

But the warm memories faded as Paul recalled how the black cloud of civil war moved closer. He remembered serious discussions around the dinner table as reports filtered to Nanking of the communist takeover of one city after another moving down closer to the Yangtze River which bisects China into north and south. Some said this was a different breed of communism—not the Russian kind that hated Christianity—but they would "probably not permit Bible schools and seminaries." Others said it would be dangerous to have anything to do with "Western imperialists" and Western missionaries if the communists were in charge. Even Western money would be tainted.

Prices skyrocketed—the nationalist government began issuing money in CN five thousand and CN ten thousand denominations. Then rice grew scarce. Refugees who fled into Nanking told of the destruction of family life under communists; the confiscation of land, forced communal living and the insults to the aged.

The communist threat drew inexorably closer as the national army withdrew in disarray.

As the train rolled on through the night, Paul remembered another journey. In December, 1948, Pastor Chang closed the rented house in Nanking and took his student body of seventy to Changsha just before all the rail lines to the south were cut off.

For a few months the seminary shared the facilities of the Hu Nang Bible School, but in June, when the military threatened to take over the campus, they had to move again.

This time all transportation was taken over by fleeing government officials and their families. Pastor Chang carefully instructed his dwindling student body on where to meet. The Christian Alliance Bible School in Kweilin had agreed to allow them to use temporarily an upper floor of their building. The students and staff were divided into small groups, each to fend for themselves until they were reunited in Kweilin.

Pastor Chang himself traveled with six of his keenest students, determined to take advantage of every minute to teach and disciple along the way. They managed to get on a train for a short distance, only to be sidetracked and left standing in the railway yard for over a week while the military took precedence.

For Paul the train ride out of Changsha the next day was like none he'd ever been on before. Refugees had swarmed onto the railway platform, clamoring for space on the train, the last out of Changsha, so that every available space was covered with people—on the roofs, in between on the couplings; some had even placed boards on the frames under the cars and were lying down in the cramped space.

Paul was glad his mother wasn't there to see him off as he pushed his way through the crowd, trying to get close enough to the train to get on. He managed to squeeze up behind the engine in front of the coal car where the black soot from the boiler almost immediately covered him from head to toe. But the engineer demanded payment for the "choice" spot and forced him off when he told him he didn't have any money.

There was a sense of panic in his heart as he moved through the crowded platform again. Every car was full. A woman was frantically calling the name of a child she'd lost, her voice drowned in the noise and confusion. A young couple tried to gather their belongings, which had fallen out of a battered case and were being trampled under hundreds of feet.

Paul would have stopped to help, but the train whistle suddenly pierced the air as the first piston stroke thrust the engine forward, straining under its load. Suddenly someone grabbed his arm and pushed him forward, "Grab the stair rail as it goes by, Paul: we'll jump onto the outside step." Paul was relieved to see that Arthur, another seminary student, had found him in the crowd.

The two held onto the stair rails of the coach as the train gathered momentum. The wind whipped their thin raincoats, and particles of soot stung their faces. It was clear why no one else had taken this perch. But now that they were here, they hung on for dear life, knowing there was no other space on this last train for Kweilin.

Arthur yelled to Paul over the noise of the wind, "We'll have to hang on until the next stop. I've got a rope in my bag so we can tie ourselves on the steps for the night."

For two weeks Paul and Arthur rode on the steps of the refugee train, chilled to the bone at night; sometimes soaked to the skin as the rain pelted them; always black with soot and dust. In the night they "stood watch" over each other—one fitfully sleeping by resting his head against the coach, his body straining at the rope that bound them to the train; the other pinching him awake if he began to slip.

One morning they heard a terrible wailing coming from under their coach. At the next stop when everyone clambered off for water and toileting, they heard that a woman had become so sleepy she'd dropped her baby during the night, and it had fallen to its death under the wheels of the train.

Another day several people were crushed to death on top of the coach when the train went through a low tunnel. Hundreds of people lost their lives on the journey.

Day after day the boys kept up their spirits by singing hymns, quoting Scripture to each other, and thanking God for each day that He spared their lives. Over and over as the beautiful scenery of China sped past them, Paul recited, "I will lift up mine eyes to the hills, from whence cometh my help." A very real sense of God's presence and help surrounded him, and he was conscious of the prayers of his family.

Paul remembered the final rain-soaked night when he'd huddled by the side of the road to get a few hours' sleep.

The Chinese countryside was overflowing with refugees fleeing south, a step ahead of the conquering communist armies. Food was scarce; prices had quadrupled in just a few months. Parents were separated from children; army deserters attacked and robbed. Morale had totally disintegrated, and it was each person for himself.

What a relief to his parents when he and his friend straggled into the CMA compound in Kweilin, the last group to be accounted for. How they praised God for His loving care and faithfulness.

Though they felt safe for the moment, there were new problems. Funds to operate the school had come primarily from the West through the Shanghai office of the China Native Evangelistic Crusade (CNEC).

But Western support was being restricted. Pastor Chang had long expected this would happen, and had been urging that the school find ways to become totally independent. Now there was no other option. In fact more than one Western missionary considered Pastor Chang "anti-Western" because of his strong emphasis on independence, particularly in matters of administration and policy decisions. One remarked, "He wants our money and support, but not our name."

But now the issue was settled for Tai Tung Seminary—if it were to carry on, it would have to find a way to support itself. Paul remembered how he and other students sat by the roadside, peddling their watches and old clothing—clothing they could ill afford to sell—just to buy food for the students.

Pastor Chang introduced industrial courses into the curriculum, and within weeks the students were making soap and handicraft products and working in the garden in the afternoons to help keep the school afloat. There was an unrealistic air of permanency about the school while the Red armies marched ever closer to Kweilin.

Suddenly the train jerked to a halt, bringing Paul back to the present, 1979. He bolted up from the bunk, an inexplicable fear clutching his throat. His memories had been so vivid, it took him a moment to realize where he was. Rubbing a spot on the steamed-up window, he saw they had come into a small town—the name on the station, like so many names in China now—was unfamiliar. In a moment the lone disembarking passenger had disappeared down the platform, and the train renewed its journey into the night. Paul noted a faint touch of color in the east—the new day would soon be dawning—and his heart leaped with praise to his heavenly Father, who was answering his prayer of thirty years.

He realized with chagrin that he was still clutching his coat protectively in both arms—an automatic gesture when the train stopped and woke him from his reveries. How often over the years had a train ride done this to him—causing him to relive that terrible ride out of Changsha to the safety of Kweilin. As the train started to move again, Paul settled back to the hypnotic sounds of the wheels rushing into the night and let his memories sweep over him once more.

The school had been in Kweilin only three months when, early in 1949, Pastor Chang called Paul into his study. His mother was sitting in the corner quietly weeping, and Paul knew his father had reached a serious decision.

"Son, we're not running anymore," he began. Paul could see his strong warm face straining to maintain control as he put his hand on his shoulder. "We've heard reports that the communist forces will overrun Kweilin in just a few weeks.

Already every available means of transport has been commandeered by the retreating nationalists. We can't move the school anymore—there are no safe places left."

Paul looked into his father's warm brown eyes and the strong face that had inspired confidence and commitment in so many of his students. He knew in his heart before a word was uttered that he was being sent away—this time for good.

"Your older brothers have families, and they have chosen to stay here, and we cannot send the twins away alone at their age. But you are seventeen and a strong Christian, and I believe God wants to use you in His work. When this is all over, China will need men of God trained in His Word and able to teach others. Therefore, we've decided to send you to Hong Kong."

Paul's father arranged passage on one of the junks moving slowly downriver to Canton, and once again Paul found himself jammed together with panic stricken refugees fleeing before the feared communist army. He arrived in Hong Kong feeling very lost and alone among the hoards of people, never dreaming it would be thirty years before he could return to his homeland.

———

As the train neared Guilin the sun was shining brightly. Paul saw again the breath-taking grandeur of the "pointed" mountains of the area. Surprisingly the countryside had changed very little in the thirty years since he'd left; but he knew the people had changed a great deal. His father Chang was dead, and Paul knew that was one sad story he would have to hear. Bits and pieces had come through to him over the years, though letters from China were always carefully worded and left much to the imagination.

In the early years while Paul was going to high school and Bible school in Hong Kong, he had heard occasionally from his father. Then his brother wrote in 1962 that his father had died. There were rumors that he had been imprisoned; a report had also been published in a Peking newspaper entitled "Changes in My Thoughts" over his father's name.

Many Christian leaders were put through intensive periods of "re-education," and though Pastor Chang never renounced his faith, he condescended to write these words: "I will stand with the great mass and obey the leadership of Chairman Mao, root out all anti-revolutionary activities that eternal peace and blessing and happiness may soon materialize in this great and democratic China, so rich in resources."

Paul recalled with bitterness the six years of the Cultural Revolution when he heard not a word from or about his family in China. During this time thousands of Christians were imprisoned, tortured, and killed, and he could only cling to the hope that his family had been spared.

Many years later his family felt safe enough to tell him the truth about his father's death. Pastor Chang had been given a ten-year sentence of hard labor and had died after three years in prison.

In turn, Paul's family knew nothing of God's care for him. All the years in Hong Kong he had been helped through the student scholarship program of CNEC with funds from Western Christians; then he worked his way through Seattle Pacific College in Washington; and earned his masters degree in music at Golden Gate Seminary. He had been in concert all over North America and even in Australia, selling his records by the thousands, and his mother had never heard him sing.

He smiled in anticipation of giving her the tape recorder and tapes of his music that he'd been able to bring into China for her, and especially the Chinese Bible with big print.

But he was sure her greatest joy would be to hear that he was a minister of the gospel, just as his father had wished. And not only that, but he was heading a great mission program out of Singapore in association with CNEC, which shared the truth of the gospel with thousands in Thailand, Indonesia, Malaysia and Burma.

She would hardly believe that CNEC—which she'd known as just a little mission helping Chinese evangelists in China—was today a worldwide mission, helping more than fifteen hundred national leaders in almost forty countries.

And Father—bless his memory—would sagely approve of CNEC (now known as Christian Nationals Evangelism Commission) policies to "provide funds and support and not expect them to use our name or accept our control," as he had so audaciously suggested more than thirty years ago.

The train pulled into Guilin—the same city he had left thirty years ago under such different circumstances. As he jumped onto the platform, he wondered if he would recognize his brother in this mass of humanity where everyone dressed the same. Suddenly he saw a familiar smiling face coming towards him. And then there were three others gathering around him—all four of his brothers reaching out to hug and greet him, tears flowing unashamedly. He had not even dared hope they would be able to meet him.

By special dispensation the three brothers working in other cities had been granted time off to be with Paul. The Chang brothers are highly respected in their communities and hold responsible positions. One is a teacher, another a basketball coach, the third a doctor, and the fourth a professor in metallurgy. And all remained true to the Lord through the long years of persecution.

The five brothers piled into a van that one of them had been able to borrow from the local hospital where his wife works, and they drove to the apartment where Paul's mother lives with her oldest son and his wife.

When they stopped in front of the building, a brother told Paul, "We live on the third floor. Mother can get up and down, but at eighty-one she has to take it pretty slowly. She's up there waiting for you." Then he added understandingly, "We'll wait down here while you go up."

As Paul bounded up the stairs, the package containing the big Bible under his arm, thirty years dropped away. He was once again the seventeen-year-old boy calling out, "Mother, I'm home."

Months later he described this poignant meeting in a letter to his friends: "My mother was waiting for me near the kitchen door. We couldn't say anything for a long time. We both just cried. Then she prayed and thanked the Lord for bringing her son back and for guiding and using him as His servant. This had been my mother's prayer over these many years. When the others joined us, we closed the door, and the whole family prayed to our Heavenly Father.

"Those days together were precious—we had family prayer and studied the Bible together. We sang many of our old, old songs that my parents taught us. My brother played the accordion. We sang duets and read Scriptures. Once my mother took a little piece of paper from her pocket to show me, saying, 'This used to be my Bible.' It was all she'd had for fifteen years. I gave her a new Bible with big letters. She told me that was the most precious gift I brought for her.

"For three days and three nights we chatted about old times and I caught up with the news of each of my brother's family. I found my mother very healthy at the age of eighty-one and my brothers have good jobs. I thanked the Lord for His goodness and mercy toward the family."

The Lord had shown goodness and mercy towards Paul over those years too. After he completed his studies in the U.S.A., Paul and his wife, Nien-Chang, returned to Hong Kong where he pastored a church and developed an effective youth ministry. In 1975 *Christian Nationals* asked him to serve in Singapore, where today he leads a multifaceted ministry of churches, correspondence courses and a cassette tape lending program, which has prepared thousands of Chinese tapes.

As Southeast Asia coordinator for *Christian Nationals Evangelism Commission,* Paul is one of several area coordinators directly responsible to *Christian Nationals,* coordinating the assistance offered to national ministries. But the administration of the mission stops there. The rest of the fifteen hundred nationals associated with the mission serve directly under national boards who set policy, establish budgets, and appoint staff.

Paul's concern for the Chinese "in the dispersion" (Chinese living in countries outside mainland China) has driven him to encourage missions in the Singapore churches. His travels into northern Thailand, Burma and West Kalimantan (formerly Borneo) have brought him into touch with national Christians struggling to spread the gospel in their corner of the vineyard. Through Paul's encouragement, the Dyaks (aborigines in the interior of Borneo) now have a training program, family camps, and several church planters working among them. He has encouraged Singapore Christians to become involved in a Sponsor-A-Child program (an education ministry of *Christian Nationals*) in northern Thailand, and to help support several Chinese evangelists as they establish churches in refugee villages and, cross-culturally, to the unreached tribal people. When he learned of the work of a team of Burmese evangelists ministering along the Chinese border, witnessing in villages where Christ had never been named, he encouraged Singapore Christians and other friends of *Christian Nationals* to meet some of the needs of this team.

Wherever he goes among the Chinese in the dispersion, Paul can communicate in their language, understand their culture, enjoy their customs, empathize with their problems—and, above all, share the truths of Scripture so they are relevant to their needs.

Throughout the Third World there are men and women, like Paul Chang, who have been evangelized and trained because of the faithfulness of Western missionaries. Today we see the fruit of their labors in second and third generation Christians, like Paul, who have themselves shouldered the burdens of building the church around the world as responsible "family" members.

2

HAVE MISSIONS PAID OFF?

When the Bamboo Curtain fell in 1950, China was cut off from the rest of the world.

Hundreds of missionaries fled before the communists, while churches were turned into warehouses and "comfort stations." Bibles were burned; Christians were paraded through the streets wearing "dunce caps." Thousands died for their faith. Great preachers and Bible teachers such as Watchman Nee and Wang Ming-dao (the Billy Graham of China) were imprisoned. Nee died in prison; Ming-dao was released, broken in body but praising God after twenty-two years of confinement.

And the church? We were sure it was dead.

After all, Christianity had never really taken root in China. It was considered a Western religion, propagated by "foreign devils."

Even Kenneth Scott Latourette, the great church historian, wrote in 1965, "Because Christianity had been associated with . . . imperialism and colonialism, the revolt might have been expected to lead to the waning of the Christian communities as alien enclaves . . . that was the case on the mainland of China."[1]

But in reality that was *not* the case in mainland China.

With the reopening of communications between China and the West in the late 1970s, news of a living, vibrant church began reaching us—Christians meeting secretly in house churches; hilltop "retreats" where believers met after straggling up the hill in twos and threes so no one would know they were gathering.

Some contact had continued. For example, a Chinese evangelist from outside China frequently slipped across the border as early as two years before the death of Mao Tse Tung in 1976, to baptize ten, twenty, thirty believers and shared his encouraging news with a small circle of friends.

Once borders were opened, travelers began bringing back stories of miracles reminding us of the early church—reports of healings and even raising from the dead.

In Thailand in June, 1980, at the Consultation on World Evangelization, delegates from around the world heard amazing reports of the church in China numbering upwards of five million (five times what it was when the revolutionary forces drove the missionaries out). Today there are an estimated twenty-five to fifty million Christians who have been meeting in more than five hundred thousand house churches. By 1983 more than four hundred official "Three-Self" churches had been reopened.

Who planted the seed? The pre-1950 missionaries.

Who watered it? The Holy Spirit through the national Christians.

A Success Story of Missions

The success of missionary work is not determined by the number of missionaries, the value of property, or the highly developed organizational structures—but by the church that is planted, takes root, and grows in that society.

All around the world today the church is becoming an integral part of society as a result of the seeds planted by faithful missionaries on the front lines and faithful prayer partners "holding the ropes."

Every day of the year it is estimated that sixty thousand people are converted to Christianity; every week about twelve hundred new churches are started.

In 1900 the African population was only three percent Christian; some twenty thousand Africans a day are converting to Christianity. If the church continues to grow at its present rate, forty-eight percent will be Christian by the turn of the century.

The church in Korea is planting six new churches every day. In Brazil the annual growth rate of the Protestant community is 6 percent, more than twice the population growth (2.8 percent).

Missionaries have not only planted churches, but developed an education system. Until recently more than eighty-five percent of the school children in Africa were in Christian schools. All over the Third World hundreds of colleges and seminaries have been established to train leaders for the growing church. Radio stations, medical programs, relief and development are all part of a ministry of love and concern carried out by some fifty-five thousand Protestant, and forty-five thousand Catholic missionaries.

A Modern Development

It was only in the mid-1940s that the fulcrum of missions shifted from European to North American churches. In 1793 the British Baptists agreed, reluctantly at first, to send William Carey to India. Carey was so persistent in his obsession with the Great Commission that in a conference one of the church leaders impatiently interrupted his pleadings to send missionaries: "Young man, sit down. When God pleases to convert the heathen, He will do it without your aid or mine." However, God used Carey to "convert the heathen" for more than forty years, and he became known as the father of modern missions.

There were other great missionary movements in Europe, such as the Moravians, before Carey, but the first American missionaries did not leave the New World until 1812, when Adoniram Judson and his companions sailed for India. Judson was ordered out of India and moved on to begin his great work in Burma.

Michael Griffiths describes the limited extent of mission work in the early nineteenth century:

At the time of William Carey's mission, David Livingston was not even born. Mofatt had not yet arrived in Africa. There were no Protestant missionaries in Latin America at all . . . in the Philippines, Taiwan, Japan, Korea, Thailand or Indo-China . . . One suddenly realizes with devastating force that 162 years ago [1810] there were scarcely any known Protestant missionaries to the Third World, let alone national Christians.[2]

However, following on the heels of the colonizing nations, Western missionaries from Europe and the New World established beachheads for Christ in many parts of the world during the nineteenth century.

With the rise of liberalism and the destructive World War in 1914, mission interest waned. Even so, by the end of the first World War, the major base of missions had shifted from Europe to the New World.

The Great Depression also slowed growth. But in the twenty-five years after the second World War, seventy-one Third World nations gained their freedom from the grip of Western domination. As nations gained independence from the colonizers and achieved their own nationhood, the subservience to Western influence diminished. The automatic acceptance of everything from the West now came under the scrutiny of nations that were developing self-esteem and national pride.

But in spite of this shift in power, the same twenty-five years became the high point of Western missions. More than one hundred new agencies were formed, and dozens of fields enlarged—this was the day of the "faith mission." In 1946 the combined agencies belonging to EFMA (Evangelical Foreign Missions Association) and IFMA (Inter-denominational Foreign Missions Association) equaled 40; by 1969, 104 agencies belonged, more than half of these founded after World War II.

In the midst of this period, Latourette observed[3] that Christianity was continuing to spread and was more widely represented than any other religion had ever been. Christians were coming together in a global fellowship embracing both westerners and non-westerners as had not been done previously. At the Lausanne Congress in 1974, for instance, the largest single bloc of delegates came from Africa.

The Church began to experience the sense of togetherness in a "worldwide family" in the great mission heyday that emerged after the second World War. Much of this was accomplished through the willingness of dedicated men and women of God to leave their homes and their familiar culture, to live and serve among people of different languages, customs, and color, for Christ's sake.

Because of this great movement of God's servants into the far-flung corners of the world, the Church is alive and growing, rooted in many cultures, multiplying itself and reaching out to others. It is estimated that out of a population of 4.2 billion there are between 1 billion and 1.2 billion people who consider themselves Christians today, and the base of evangelicalism has swung from the West to the Third World.

Is the Job of Missions Completed?

With such phenomenal growth in recent years, should we consider the task completed?

By no means.

Reporting on the Thailand Consultation in *Decision* magazine, Roger Palms wrote, "By the year 2000 the population will have grown to approximately seven billion, with 5.2 billion not knowing the message of Jesus Christ . . . 20 years from now there will be more people in the world who have never responded to the message of Jesus than there are people in the world today."[4]

The U.S. Center for World Mission is dedicated to the task of arousing concern and training missionaries to reach the "unreached groups"—the 2.7 billion people who cannot hear the gospel from anyone within their group. Including the three major blocs—the Chinese (1 billion), Hindus (650 million), and Muslims (700 million)—these total some seventeen thousand distinct people groups. Less than ten percent of the Western mission force works among these unreached peoples. Thus the clarion call of "200,000 missionaries by the year 2000" made at Thailand presents some formidable challenges for foreign missions from both the West and the Third World, as the developing churches awaken to their part in world missions.

Politically, many of the world's most needy areas are also the most resistant to foreign missionaries. For some time, India has restricted the entrance of new professional missionaries, and the resident foreign missionary force has diminished by forty percent in the last fifteen years. Though veteran missionaries are permitted to remain, new visas tend to be limited to specialists who cannot be substituted by Indians themselves. Mrs. Gandhi has long reiterated that religions should be propagated by Indians themselves.

Burma was closed to all foreign missionaries in 1966, and it has been difficult for foreigners even to obtain a visitor's visa.

Brazil, which was one of the most wide-open mission countries, with more than three thousand foreign missionaries, has recently restricted the issuance of visas to new resident missionaries.

More than forty countries are closed or seriously restrict foreign mission work by law (see map).

However, even where not politically restricted, foreigners, and particularly Americans, are not readily accepted in many countries. Latin Americans have long resented "Yankee imperialism," and missionaries have come under the same condemnation in many instances.

Stephen Neill, veteran British missionary to India, and author and lecturer, in an interview with *Christianity Today*, says: "Third World churches have come to detest the words 'mission' and 'missionary.' It is our fault; we've held on too long. To them 'mission' and 'missionary' implies western aggression, western authoritarianism, the stifling of local independence."[5]

A student from Sri Lanka was quoted as saying, "Foreign missions made a type of 'evangelical robot' out of us."

Not only are political restrictions and nationalistic attitudes limiting the effectiveness of foreign missionaries in some areas, but the decadence of the West has made it vital to disassociate Christianity from Western society. Iran's abhorrence of the ethical and moral standards of "Christian" America some years ago—when its religious leaders actually wanted to protect its people from contact with our way of life—is an extreme example of how this attitude can restrict the effectiveness of Western missionaries.

In spite of these limitations there are greater oppor-

38

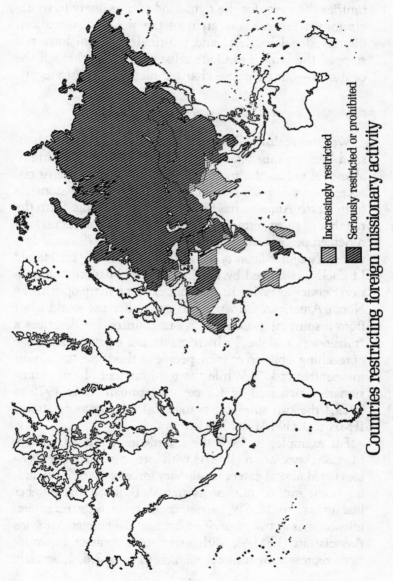

Countries restricting foreign missionary activity

Increasingly restricted

Seriously restricted or prohibited

tunities than ever for the right kind of missionary in strategic ministries in many areas of the world. Persecution, distrust, legal barriers, and political upheaval have not stopped the growth of God's mission program through the centuries—but they *have* changed methods and strategy!

How Shall They Be Sent?

We must realistically face the fact that two hundred thousand Western missionaries by the year 2000 is an unattainable goal unless the interest and involvement in missions accelerates rapidly. The total number of career missionaries from North America has been steadily increasing. With the number of short-termers included, there was an increase of nineteen percent in the years from 1975 to 1979, according to the *Twelfth Edition of the Mission Handbook*. Yet Harold Lindsell was quoted by the Evangelical Missions Information Service as saying he does not expect a sharp upswing by North American Christians to evangelize the world apart from a spiritual awakening in our country. He describes a "missionary malaise," which makes the gigantic challenge of reaching a billion or more people in the 1980s "an almost insuperable task."[6] While the total number of career missionaries increased by 3.5 percent annually from 1976 to 1979,[7] the two strongest evangelical mission associations, IFMA and EFMA, did not fare as well.

For example, in 1978 the Interdenominational Foreign Mission Association (IFMA) with forty-nine member agencies listed a total career missionary force of 10,662 (including home staff on missionary status). By 1980 that number had grown to 10,679, a net increase of only seventeen missionaries in two years. The Evangelical Foreign Missions Association (EFMA), with eighty-one member organizations representing a career mission force of 7,632, actually declined by two tenths of one percent over that period of time. Though many mainline denominational mission boards show a decline, the Foreign Mission Board of the Southern Baptist convention continues to grow. However while the number of short-term "volunteers" jumped twenty-seven percent in 1980, and the total missionary force increased by two percent, the *number of career missionaries rose by only two persons*, according to a news release issued by the board in February of 1981.

Even if the personnel were available, the rising cost of sending Western missionaries continues to accelerate. Harold Ockenga, president emeritus of Gordon Conwell Seminary, expresses this concern:

As a pastor for forty years, I led a church which supported 142 missionaries at a cost of $250,000 a year. Today, that same church supports seventy-two missionaries and spends $510,000 or $7,000 per person. How many local congregations can maintain a missionary enthusiasm when the sending of a missionary couple to Latin America, India, or Europe costs more than the congregation pays its own pastors?[8]

At present, many mission agencies estimate it costs an average of $30,000 a year to maintain a missionary family on the field, and even more in such "high cost" areas as Europe. At a moderate rate of six percent inflation this would come to more than $118,000 a year by the year 2000—and we would need almost six times the present number to reach the goal. When one considers that the present total budget for missions in North America is less than $1.5 billion, one realizes a supplementary plan for world evangelization would be wise.

A Supplementary Plan

In our discussion of missions we have dealt primarily with the need to increase our Western missionary force. But Third World missionaries are already making a tremendous contribution. It is estimated that more than thirteen thousand Third World missionaries are serving around the world, representing a more than 282 percent increase from 1972 to 1980.[9] If we also include the growing corps of trained national Christians ready to serve Christ among their own unreached peoples or nearby culture, the goal of two hundred thousand can be more easily reached.

These "new cross-cultural missionaries" face formidable challenges, such as tribal and national barriers of language, and traditional hostilities. Still, in most cases, a ready acceptance has been demonstrated by fellow Third World people groups.

However, if they're going to go, they'll need assistance just as Western missionaries do. In many instances, the nationals are willing and ready to serve, but lack the financial base.

Consider the ten thousand Korean young people who volunteered for mission work at the great evangelistic gathering in 1980. Though the Korean church is growing at an astounding rate (six new churches established daily), it is far beyond the capacity of that church to send out ten thousand workers into all the world. Even if one considers that they would live on one quarter of what a Western missionary needs ($625 a month, compared to $2500), to send ten thousand Koreans would be 6.25 million dollars a month ($75 million a year). Though Korean Christians are already supporting many missionaries (in spite of currency restrictions that limit the sending out of funds), it will be some time before they are able to support such a large number of missionaries, and Western assistance will be needed.

The idea of foreign support for national workers has been around for a long time. Many have questioned whether there is a biblical basis for this strategy. Some explain that Paul planted self-supporting churches from the beginning, and that he never asked for funds to support a church in another area.

Others have raised serious questions about the wisdom of supporting nationals, pointing out the tremendous dangers and inherent weaknesses documented by sad experiences.

In the following chapters we will address ourselves to these questions: Is there a biblical basis for helping nationals? Can the frustrations and dangers be overcome? Has helping nationals worked?

Notes

1. Kenneth Scott Latourette, *Missions Tomorrow,* Harper and Brothers, New York, 1936, p. 127, 130.
2. James Wong; Peter Larson, *Mission from the Third World,* Church Growth Study Center, Singapore, 1973.
3. Kenneth Scott Latourette, *Christianity in a Revolutionary Age,* Harper & Row, New York, Vol. 5, 1962, p. 526.
4. Roger C. Palms, "3,000,000,000 People How Shall They Hear?" *Decision,* Billy Graham Evangelistic Association, October, 1980.
5. Stephen Neill, "Building the Church on Two Continents," *Christianity Today,* July 18, 1980, pp. 18-23.
6. "A New Era," *Evangelical Missions Information Service,* 1980 Annual Report, annual board meeting, December 11, 1980, p. 1.
7. Samuel Wilson, editor, *Twelfth Edition Mission Handbook,* Missions Advanced Research and Communication Center, Monrovia, CA, 1979, p. 25.
8. J. Christy Wilson, *Today's Tentmakers: Self Support an Alternative Model for Worldwide Witness,* Tyndale House Publishers, Wheaton, IL, 1979, p. 9.,
9. Lawrence E. Keyes, *The Last Age of Missions,* William Carey Library, Pasadena, CA, 1983, p. 62.

3

WHAT DOES THE BIBLE SAY ABOUT HELPING NATIONALS?

The old pastor stood up at the end of the prayer meeting—"Brethren," he began, "while we've been praying for someone to go to the Giriamas, the Lord has spoken to me." Then he paused as if just now realizing the seriousness of his decision, "I will go."

So it was that Josiah Mutiandi, a pastor of the indigenous Africa Inland Church (AIC) in Kenya, became the first Kamba missionary to go to the Giriamas—a primitive tribe that had for centuries resisted all efforts by Islam, Christianity, and even Western civilization, to make inroads among them. Living on the hot, dusty, coastal plains, the Giriamas spent much of their time brewing palm wine. Every rite of passage became an extended orgy. There were no schools for their children, no medical facilities, no churches. Their huts were made of crudest thatch and mud; in the heat they needed and wore little clothing. Even the shelter over their wooden gods in the middle of the village had fallen into disarray. They seemed to be a people without purpose or progress.

Pastor Mutiandi left his family behind on the cooler highlands and moved to one of the Giriama villages, sharing their simple interests and modeling the life of Christ.

But the Giriamas were resistant, and it was only after he was able to arrange help for a pregnant woman in a complicated delivery that the villagers began to listen to his message, and a village church was established.

44

The Africa Inland Church was able to send several other pastors, who left the high, cooler plateaus, to live and work in the lowlands. Even though life was difficult in the hot, dry, barren region, there was no shortage of volunteers, but there was a shortage of funds.

One pastor working among the Giriamas wrote:

My heart is determined to serve the Lord, but lack of money makes my effort in vain. . . . If my money cannot maintain me, it's needless to mention about my family (eight children). Only God can know how they can manage to live on their own while I am at the coast some hundreds of kilometers away. The money I get cannot make me live with my family. Everything remains in the hands of God.

Although the church members were struggling to support their missionaries to the Giriamas, they saw for the first time the growing responsiveness in the hearts of the Giriama people. If only they could send more pastors *and* their families to live among the villagers.

And so it was in 1974 that Reverend Mulwa, then head of the AIC churches in Kenya, presented the needs of the Giriama tribe to *Christian Nationals.* The Africa Inland Church, an indigenous body of churches that had grown out of the work of the Africa Inland Mission, had pioneered outreach into eight other unreached tribes and had little support available for new workers. "But," wrote Reverend Mulwa, "if we had ten more missionaries, we could evangelize much more of the tribe. It takes about $50 a month to support a national to take the Gospel to the Giriama people."

Christian Nationals gained help for ten workers, and within several years a dozen churches were established, and four young Giriamas were in Bible school preparing to return to minister to their own people.

Was it right to send help from the outside to assist these

Kenyan missionaries so they could go to work among the Giriamas? What does Scripture have to say about assisting a pastor like the one who wrote the letter concerning his financial need?

"Whoever sees his brother in need"

We know that we have passed from death to life, because we love our brothers. . . . If anyone has material possessions and sees his brother in need but has no pity on him, how can the love of God be in him? Dear children, let us not love with words or tongue but with actions and in truth. (1 John 3:14–18)

John raises the burning issue of love for the brethren (fellow Christians). He pinpoints the mark of true discipleship: "We know that we have passed from death to life because we love our brothers." He is echoing the teaching of Jesus who said, "All men will know that you are my disciples if you love one another" (John 13:35).

John follows his statement that we know we are in God's family because we love the brothers with a very practical question. How can we deny part of our "family" the very necessities of life if we have plenty, and they are in need? How can we close our hearts to them? John urges us to go beyond words (God bless you, brother) to actions (Here, please have a share of what I have). Then he clearly states that this principle is *the* truth. This implies we must go a step further by sharing because it is *right*, and not just because there is a need.

The Giriama pastor was certainly "in need"—he could not even keep his family with him because he did not have the means to do so. And it was scripturally "right" to help him!

The Family Tie

In this day of mass communication and satellite transmission, the responsibility becomes awesome, for we *see* so much need all over the world. To a degree, it has always been true that there are so many more needs around us than we can ever hope to meet. The church throughout the ages has taken the responsibility to communicate special needs to the "family." The Apostle Paul wrote to the church in Galatia that "as we have opportunity, let us do good to all people, especially to those who belong to the family of believers" (Gal. 6:10).

Paul had experienced that truth in action while he was teaching in the newly formed church in Antioch in the nation of Syria. There had been some cultural tensions between this predominantly Gentile congregation and Jewish Christians in Judea, the nation to the south. But when Agabus came and told the brethren in Antioch about the needs of the Judean Christians because of a drought in their area, the disciples "decided to provide help for the brothers"—this they did, each one giving as much as he could, consigning their gifts to Barnabas and Paul to take to the elders at Jerusalem (Acts 11:28,29). It is important to note that the gifts were sent in an orderly fashion from church board to church board (elders) who in turn distributed them to the needy in their area.

And so the very first church established outside Judea practiced the principle of sharing within the "family." Though they were in a different nation (Syria) and a different culture (Gentile), they recognized the Jewish believers in Judea as their brothers, and since they "saw their brothers in need," and they had enough material possessions, they loved in deed and truth by sending real help—not just words of blessing.

47

It is little wonder that several years later Paul commended the Corinthians for their spirit of readiness and their desire to help needy Christians in another country (2 Cor. 9:2). He knew he could depend upon their response when he sent Titus to them for the collection of their gifts of assistance. For us today this demands a spirit of willingness to respond to need as it comes to our attention, rather than resenting what we see as a bombardment of requests.

James spoke strongly against the "misuse of riches."

Your wealth has rotted, and moths have eaten your clothes. Your gold and silver are corroded. Their corrosion will testify against you and eat your flesh like fire. You have hoarded wealth in the last days. Look! The wages you failed to pay the workmen who mowed your fields are crying out against you. The cries of harvesters have reached the ears of the Lord, Almighty. You have lived on earth in luxury and self-indulgence. . . . You have condemned and murdered innocent men, who were not opposing you (James 5:2–6).

John goes further by warning that in the lack of love are the seeds of death: "We know that we have passed from death to life, because we love our brothers" (1 John 3:14). There are many ways to "slay our brother." Can it be that by closing our hearts against our brothers and sisters who are in need when we could have helped them we have contributed to their death?

On the other hand, when needs are presented to us through God's channels, and we are ready to obey His leading, then the Spirit of God will strike a chord of response in our own hearts when He wants us to become involved in a particular work or area of need. This was Titus's experience, for Paul explains to the Corinthians, "I thank God, who put into the heart of Titus the same concern I have for you" (2 Cor. 8:16).

"Let Them Help Themselves" Syndrome

The church was born in a Jewish society and needed to be delivered from the sin of pride of race and culture from its beginning. Unfortunately this sin also afflicts the church in the West. Pride of race and culture causes self-centeredness. We accept members of our local church, or even our denomination, as "our family"—for whose needs we have a God-given responsibility. But we look at Christians in other countries as "foreigners" who should be responsible for their own needs.

Missionary Kenneth Donald, who worked in India for twenty-seven years and was troubled by such inconsistency, asks, "Can we really justify some new palatial 'home' church buildings in the West, while we stipulate that a poor illiterate villager, heavily in debt, must give out of his meager earnings just to keep his own little mud and thatch church going?"[1]

No Foreigners in the Family of God

The story of Peter's visit to Cornelius' home in Caesarea (Acts 10) is a lesson in family awareness.

We can picture the scene: Peter, a proud, impetuous Jew, standing in a Gentile's home filled with Romans; sitting nearby is Cornelius, a man with a devout heart, seeking God. At first Peter would not have entered a Gentile home, but God rebuked him. Now when Peter preached, the same Gentiles turned to Christ. It is said that the Jewish believers who came with Peter "were astonished that the gift of the Holy Spirit had been poured out even on the Gentiles" (Acts 10:45).

Peter and his co-workers had begun to learn that there are no foreigners in God's family. That lesson had to be

49

taught to the church as a whole when Peter later returned to Jerusalem to appear before the church leaders to defend his actions of going into a Gentile home.

We are still learning that the family of God includes men and women from every nation of the world. The household of faith is multiracial, and our responsibility includes them all.

The Kenyan church gave the opportunity to "do good" to those self-sacrificing African national missionaries who left home, family, their own culture, language, and the appreciative response of their Kamba congregations, to work among unreached Giriamas, but they needed the help of the wider family of God. Brothers and sisters across the sea saw that need and responded in love.

Inequities Equalized

When Paul also encouraged the Corinthian Christians to take an offering, he focused on equality. "Our desire is not that others might be relieved while you are hard pressed, but that there might be equality. At the present time your plenty will supply what they need, so that in turn their plenty will supply what you need. Then there will be equality" (2 Cor. 8:13,14).

Certainly Paul was referring to financial equality in this verse. But equality of another dimension was the issue for which the first council of the Christian church was called (Acts 15). Paul and Barnabas agreed that there were cultural distinctions within the church, but there must not be cultural impositions. The Jerusalem leaders had insisted that Gentiles be circumcised and conform to Jewish cultural traditions if they were to be accepted.

Peter sided with Paul and Barnabas in the debate. At the council he repeated the story of his experience with Cornelius in Caesarea:

. . ."Brothers, you know that some time ago God made a choice among you that the Gentiles might hear from my lips the message of the gospel and believe. God, who knows the heart, showed that he accepted them by giving the Holy Spirit to them, just as he did to us. He made no distinction between us and them, for he purified their hearts by faith" (Acts 15:7–11).

Both Peter and Paul eloquently defended this principle of spiritual equality and cited their ministries among the Gentiles. In summation, James agreed with all that had been spoken, recognizing that it was God Himself who was concerned about "taking from the Gentiles a people for himself" (Acts 15:14).

From this point on, the church officially recognized that neither nationality, culture, nor race could deny salvation to any who believed. Therefore all are part of God's "forever family," a truth voiced in our day by the words of the song:

> We are the Family of God,
> Yes, we are the Family of God.
> And He's brought us together to be One in Him,
> That we might bring light to the World.
>
> Jon Byron *

Equality in salvation has been a basic foundation in the church and the prime force for missions. Lack of respect for others' forms of worship and outworkings of faith, however, has remained a point of contention, and still contributes to misunderstandings in the church.

For example, it was all right for Western missionaries to use pianos, accordians and pump organs in African churches (though these were also used in honky-tonks and bars in the West), but it was not permitted for Africans to use drums or other "heathen" instruments in worship, because they had been used for their heathen festivities.

When financial aid was given to national leaders to fulfill their ministry, missionaries often, unfortunately, expected them to follow the patterns of worship, church practice, accountability, lifestyles, etc., that are followed in the West. If these leaders are to be accepted as equal members of the family of God (no foreigners in the family), joint heirs with us in salvation, deserving of help from the family (out of our abundance to their lack of abundance), then we must also allow them equality in the Spirit.

All Christians are parts of the one body of which Christ is the Head. The whole body functions best when each part does its work with equal concern for one another. "There is one body and one Spirit—just as you were called to one hope when you were called—one Lord, one faith, one baptism; one God and Father of all. . . . But to each one of us grace has been given as Christ apportioned it" (Eph. 4:4,5).

The same Spirit guides, remonstrates, comforts, and convicts the church in India, Africa, and Latin America as He does the church in North America. But the methodology, form, and lifestyle may be drastically different; that is His prerogative. That we have the responsibility to assist this church is patently clear from Scripture as well as logic, as Peter Beyerhaus, missions professor, so clearly puts it:

The church which bears responsibility for missionary work in a certain area is not only the indigenous church on the spot, but . . . every Christian group in the world. In "One Body, One Gospel, One World," Leslie Newbigin shows how absurd it is that a small indigenous church, still struggling for its very existence, should be given the task of evangelizing its whole neighbourhood, while the church of the West, ready to share its strong financial and personnel resources, should be restricted to only occasional acts of assistance.[2]

Western Christians are dependent upon a large and broadly-based group of Christians to support the many programs from which we benefit (education in public schools, pastors and leaders trained in seminaries funded by others, radio and T.V. backed by gifts from across the country, camps and conference grounds built by grants, Christian colleges helped by foundations, etc.). The fact that these benefits happen to come from within the boundaries of our country does not make us totally independent. In fact, our interdependence on a broad scale makes so many of these opportunities possible. The fact that the people within these boundaries are the most affluent in the world simply points up our selfishness and self-centeredness when funds are circulated only within the country or to our countrymen rather than within the whole body.

But even when we have given—and often given generously—"Western money for Westerners" becomes the norm. This led Dr. Byang Kato to write about a comment made in humor at the Green Lake Missions Conference. "Where the American dollar is, there he must be in person. If he is not there, his dollar must not go." The suspicion is more than a point of humor to the national. Many really believe that American Christians are interested only in their own man there.[3]

Servants of All

Even while we "assist" we struggle with ingrained attitudes of superiority. Fifty years ago the great missionary statesman Roland Allen wrote:

Want of faith has made us fear and distrust native independence. We have imagined ourselves to be and have acted so as to become indispensable. . . . If anyone suggests giving to the native any freedom of action, the first thought that arises in our minds is not one of eager interest to see how they will act but one of questioning; if we allow that, how shall we prevent some horrible disaster?[4]

Thinking to protect the young church, the preaching and teaching was done by the missionaries who knew what was "right" in relation to customs. As converts caught the vision of evangelism, however, they frequently began to use methods that they felt were more effective in relating to the people.

Ed Dayton observes that a widely held misconception was that peoples of other lands, particularly non-Western peoples, were like children who needed the guidance of more sophisticated Westerners. They could not be trusted to adapt the gospel to their own cultures.

Because of this attitude many missions yielded to the pressures of pride of race and culture and refused to support or to share the supplies available from the main part of the body with the "natives who could not be trusted." To justify this, the vague principles of "self-supporting, self-propagating" were put forth as the biblical norm, while the clear biblical principle of "sharing with our brothers in need" was often violated.

Who Shall Be First?

We must confess that the servant attitude is often sadly lacking in the church. From the dawn of history, position, pride, and prominence—the heritage of the enemy—have vied with humility, service, and unselfishness.

On the other hand, Jesus taught that the true shepherd lays down his life for his sheep. He demonstrated that the way to greatness and godliness was in meekness and self-giving. He sought to teach His apostles that if they were to be great in the Kingdom, they were to be the servants of all. "But many who are first will be last, and many who are last will be first" (Matt. 19:30).

He showed them that God loved not only his special "people of the promise," but also men and women everywhere.

He would, indeed, call out from among the people, kindred tongue, and nation, a people for His name. It would be His body, made up of many parts. They would be a whole new order. They would astound the world with their self-giving love, with their acceptance and concern, as He demonstrated for the outcast leper. His truth would reach the Pharisee and the slave. His Word would penetrate every tongue and tribe. This would be the family of God with its unity and diversity. No one whom He had "cleansed would be called common." There should be no foreigners in the family of God, and they should be responsible for one another.

So, what does the Scripture say about helping the Kenyan missionaries to the Giriamas, and others like them? That as we learn of their need, our hearts should respond in love (not simply in words, but in practical action) to these members of the family of God who are as equipped by the Holy Spirit as we are to fulfill the Great Commission.

Yes, assisting nationals can be advocated from Scripture, but for many years churches and missions have held serious misconceptions about helping financially with no strings attached.

You yourself may still hold some of these mistaken impressions, consciously or subconsciously. In the following chapter we will deal with some of these misconceptions before going on to spell out workable and proven policies for assisting national leaders.

Notes

1. Kenneth Donald, "What is Wrong With Foreign Money for National Pastors?" *Evangelical Missions Quarterly*, Volume 13, Number 1, January 1977, p. 20.
2. Peter Beyerhaus, "International Review of Mission," 1964, Vol. 53:393-407. Reprinted in *Readings in Dynamic Indigeneity*, eds. Kraft and Wisley, WCL 1979, pp. 29-30.
3. *Evangelical Missions Quarterly*, Summer/1972, p. 195.
4. Allen Roland, *Missionary Methods: St. Paul's or Ours*, William B. Eerdmans Publishing Company, Grand Rapids, MI, 1962, pp. 143,144.

4

IMPRESSIONS ABOUT NATIONAL LEADERS: TRUE OR FALSE?

They call him "dynamite" because of his powerful preaching; but the night Evangelista Siodora's life was saved, it had nothing to do with any power of his own.

Siodora had traveled to a remote tribal village in a mountainous area of the Philippines to preach the gospel. But Satan had other plans, and the local witch doctor instructed one of the chiefs to take his "bolo knife" and finish off the preacher. The chief was well-practiced in this art; he'd beheaded two men just weeks before.

He stole into Siodora's room in the middle of the night and found the evangelist still awake. As he raised his arm to strike him in the neck, Siodora recounts, "Somebody held his hand . . . and the knife fell to the ground." That "Somebody" had other plans for the chief's life! He accepted Christ during that campaign and today is preaching the gospel.

Siodora loves to recount how God is working among the tribal people.

More than one hundred such primitive tribes dot the lowlands and inaccessible mountain regions of the Philippines, far from the reach of civilization. But most of the Christian workers in the country minister in the urban areas, while seventy percent of the people who live in rural and isolated parts of the country are neglected.

To meet this need a group of Filipino Christians gathered

to establish the Philippine Missionary Fellowship (PMF), in 1960, with the express purpose of reaching the unreached in every corner of this island nation. Evangelista Siodora had been involved with PMF over the years, even as he pastored churches and worked with other organizations, but in 1978 he joined the mission officially as its director.

Shortly after PMF was founded, its leaders realized that they needed a Bible school to provide practical training for rural ministries. Sending prospective missionaries into the whirl of Manila with its six million people made it difficult for young people to return to their rural calling.

In 1961 the Philippine Missionary Institute (PMI) was established. Averaging around sixty students a year, PMI has sent hundreds of young people into missionary work, many under the umbrella of PMF. More missionaries applied than could be accepted, even though candidates knew PMF missionaries lived sacrificially. Some single missionaries were given only seven to ten dollars a month while boarding with a local family in the village. Couples with children received less than one hundred dollars, and finding accommodations and educating children became serious needs. Eventually some had to resign and find other employment to care for their families, but for most the sacrifice was outstripped by the satisfying results.

Lilia Castro, for example, has an M.A. in religious education and a degree in nursing. But she chose to serve the Lord among the Mamanwa tribe in Mindanao—two and one-half days' journey by boat from Manila, another day by bus, and another four to five hours' climb up a steep mountain. "So steep," laughs Siodora, "that your knees touch your chin as you climb."

When Siodora visited Lilia, he found that five clans had come together for a service. Each clan is made up of forty to fifty people, all living in the same grass house with their dogs and pigs, and each person wearing one piece of clothing until it is worn out. But the significant thing about this meeting was not the conglomerate smells and sounds—but the fact that five warring chiefs, who had never met peaceably before in their lives, had come to be baptized together.

Yet Lilia's parents and friends find it difficult to understand why she would want to waste her life in that desolate and isolated region! When Lilia and her co-workers go back to Manila for medical care and rest, they often stay at the PMF headquarters. Until recently the headquarters consisted of a small cement block building with four little rooms, two of which were used at night as sleeping quarters for staff.

From this unimposing base the work carried on. Needs were shared with Filipino churches, and a good portion of PMF's budget came from within the country. Forty missionaries were out on the field. But by 1978 it seemed as though every resource had been tapped; the mission had reached the limit of its funds. Candidates waiting on the sidelines were put on "hold"; even the willing staff and missionaries could cut back no further to share with another in their ranks. Siodora's heart ached as he visited the islands and saw the receptivity of the people, but he could send no one to bring in the harvest.

It was then he turned to *Christian Nationals Evangelism Commission,* an agency in North America that was willing to commit financial resources to augment PMF's budget.

By 1983, 126 missionaries were serving with PMF, and more than one hundred churches were established. Once leaders are trained the missionaries move on. Siodora explains, "If the church wants to retain the missionary, he loses his status as a missionary and becomes a pastor. Then the church gradually takes over his support."

Christian Nationals was also able to help raise funds for a new headquarters building in Manila, which would adequately house the staff and provide accommodations for missionaries when they came to the city from time to time.

Yet, when a Western missionary working in the Philippines heard of the new agreement between PMF and *Christian Nationals*, the response was, "Siodora and his group have been doing a good job and have been well accepted. I certainly hope this kind of assistance doesn't spoil them!"

Almost unconsciously this missionary was reflecting the attitude that many Western Christians hold, that helping national churches financially in any way will hurt them, or that only Westerners can handle money.

Before discussing this and other misconceptions about supporting nationals further, it should be clear from the outset that it is not our intent to suggest that Western churches should send only money, and not people. The Bible does not release Christians of any culture from the responsibility of fulfilling the Great Commission. And there is much left for Western missionaries to do to evangelize unreached areas, and to disciple and train leaders, especially where the church has grown rapidly.

Gottfried Osei-Mensah, executive secretary of the Lausanne Committee for World Evangelization, warns, "I am concerned that unless we find some way of discipling and instructing the new Christians, we might be in danger in a generation or two, when we have a large body of interested people who call themselves Christians but who have not been taught."[1]

The West must continue to send workers to Africa and wherever they are needed. But the West must also understand the importance of helping the national missionary. Part of understanding is correcting wrong ideas.

True or False: You'll Spoil Them

In a classic missionary book of the fifties, *Missions at the Crossroads*, Stanley Soltau made it clear that missionaries must resist the urge to give (to the national church):

When a man comes to ask for assistance (of a missionary), he will nearly always ask for double or more than what he expects to get. Very often in doing so he is entirely unconscious of any moral defects or inconsistency in carrying out a lifetime custom. This necessitates what must often seem to the new missionary an attitude of heartless indifference at turning a deaf ear to an apparently earnest plea; yet it is one that is absolutely necessary at times in the interest of teaching the young Christians and churches to stand on their own feet and develop a spirit of independence and initiative.[2]

Experience seemed to indicate to most missionaries in those days that support would ruin or hurt the growth of the church, and that as soon as a church was established it should be self-supporting. Soltau felt very strongly that the West should not assist churches financially. The pendulum had swung to the far left, and missions were becoming exercised about the need to allow national churches to become self-supporting, self-propagating and self-governing.

Dr. James Plueddemann of the Wheaton Graduate School, however, believes the pendulum swung too far. He observes, "I'm a bit surprised at the nearsighted fear that if we help hundreds of thousands of weak, struggling churches around the world to grow toward maturity that evangelism will be hindered."

The fear of making "rice Christians" persists, however. The term, which originated in India, was used to describe some "non-caste" converts who moved out of their antagonistic communities once they became believers and settled on the mission stations. There they studied, worked, married, and worshiped within their Christian ghetto. Many were earnest believers, but some came for the benefits received from making a profession of faith—hence the term, "rice Christians."

Wrongly given, financial help certainly can make a Christian, or a church, weak and dependent. Pius Wakatama, articulate Christian leader from Zimbabwe, says in his book, *Independence for the Third World Church,* "The Biblical principle of establishing self-supporting churches is a sound one . . . this principle was not followed. Foreign funds were used in establishing and maintaining national churches overseas. The result is that the American dollar crippled indigenous initiative and saddled the churches with expensive programs which they can never dream of financing themselves."[3]

Funding wrongly given *can* create dependence and cripple the national church. Funding rightly given can create a way of escape from dependence, as we shall illustrate later on.

True or False: You Must Not Give to an Indigenous Ministry

With the emphasis on the indigenous church, the misconception developed that an indigenous national ministry cannot receive outside help.

An indigenous ministry is one that springs naturally from the soil of the culture; is rooted deeply, and thrives in the local environment; is not a "hot-house" variety that withers with the first cold breath of reality.

As long as the indigenous ministry maintains its independence, makes its own decisions, lays its own plans, without control from the outside, it can retain its indigeneity, even though it may receive help from the outside. The difficulty with our typical Western financial assistance is that controls and Western expectations or demands are attached to the gift, so that the character and scope of the ministry reflect the donor rather than the receiver.

An indigenous ministry such as PMF would not lightly jeopardize its independence and identity in order to obtain funds from a Western organization. Thus Siodora's letter to PMF's constituency explaining the relationship with *Christian Nationals* reinforced this point:

Christian Nationals will not interfere with our administration as a missionary organization. We will still be governed by our local board and operate on tested principles suitable for the Philippines. Our indigenous and autonomous character will not be affected at all. . . . We will continue to challenge churches in the Philippines to sponsor missionaries who work with us.

Help given has not curtailed local support but enhanced it, and today PMF receives sixty percent of its operating budget from within the Philippines. More Filipino missionaries than ever are planting indigenous churches in the unreached rural areas of that island nation.

True or False: You Can't Trust Younger Churches

Another widely held, though probably unadmitted, misconception in the Western church is that the churches in the non-Western world are too immature to handle money wisely. They can point to innumerable occasions when an African church treasurer "ate" the money; or where a visionary presented grandiose plans that never materialized.

1. *False Premise: Youthful Immaturity.* Yet underlying this

misconception are a number of false premises. One is that the church in the non-Western world is young; that is, it does not have a long history of experience and growth to reflect upon. It is true that modern missions date back only to the time of William Carey in the early nineteenth century.

But the church in south India, for example, claims to trace its roots back to the first century, with a strong tradition that the apostle Thomas founded the church there and was martyred in the city of Madras.

The Coptic Church in Egypt dates back to the early church fathers; the city of Alexandria in North Africa boasted of a prestigious seminary where scholars of the stature of Origen taught and wrote.

Christianity was established in Ethiopia and China during the third century. According to tradition, the gospel was taken to Arabia by the apostle Bartholomew, and it seems fairly certain that by A.D. 525 Christianity was firmly planted there.

Historian Herbert Kane summarized the spread of Christianity:

By the end of the fifth century Christianity had, with varying degrees of success, become established in all parts of the (Roman) empire, and even beyond, from the Sahara Desert in the south to Hadrian's Wall in the north, and from India in the east to Spain in the west. . . .

. . . At an early date Christianity was established in Mesopotamia and Persia. From there it spread into India, Central Asia, and China. This was the Nestorian form of Christianity. . . . In subsequent centuries the Nestorian Church became one of the greatest missionary churches of all time.[4]

By the sixth century the church had spread through Europe, North Africa, Persia, China, and India, and though this church in many instances was weak or snuffed out due to persecution or the influence of Islam, in many places a flicker of life remained. Thus the church in parts of the Third World existed for hundreds of years before the Pilgrims landed in the New World, and is, in reality, historically much older.

And what does the Western church know of maturity through suffering?

It has not been imprisoned for its faith as the Russians have, or persecuted for its courage as have Christians in Muslim countries. Its members have not died of starvation, drought and disaster as thousands of Africans in east Africa still do. It has not been ruled by a psychotic, tyrannical ruler as the Ugandan Christians have. It has not survived without Bibles, Christian literature or training facilities as have the Chinese, nor have its members had to flee their homes in a desperate run for their lives as the Cambodians.

These Christians well understand James's words of encouragement, "Consider it pure joy, my brothers, whenever you face trials of many kinds, because you know that the testing of your faith develops perseverance. . . . that you may be mature and complete, not lacking anything" (James 1:2–4).

If maturity is one of the byproducts of suffering, churches in the Third World have much to teach the West.

2. *False Premise: Small in Number.* Many hold the false premise that the Third World church is small in size. Peter Wagner reminds us that by the year 2000 approximately sixty percent of the world's Christians will be found in the Third World. Before long Christianity will no longer be considered a white man's religion. "Not that there will be fewer white feet—heaven forbid! But these white feet will be joined by a vastly increasing number of brown, black, red and yellow feet."[5]

More specificially, some of the largest local congregations in the world are in developing countries. For example, the Full Gospel Central Church in Seoul, Korea, has more than 250,000 members who meet in 10,000 small groups all over the city for Bible study and body life and gather for praise and celebration once a week. The largest crowd ever to gather for a Christian meeting came together in Seoul, Korea, on an abandoned air field in the summer of 1980, when 2¼ to 3 million people met for four days. An estimated two million people remained for an all-night prayer meeting in spite of intermittent rain.

In 1982, Guatemalan evangelicals celebrated their centennial with a massive parade in Guatemala City. Evangelist Luis Palau addressed the more than seven hundred thousand (by government count) who had gathered for the celebration.

3. *False Premise: Lacking in Leadership.* The third false premise is that the ablest and most spiritual leadership in the Christian world comes from the West. Yet at the Lausanne Congress on World Evangelization (COWE) in 1974 and the Thailand COWE in 1980 the delegates were predominantly from the Third World churches. Western finances and administrative expertise put the conference together, but a majority of the papers and reports were given by such Third World leaders as Dr. Samuel Kamaleson of India, Dr. Billy Kim of Korea, Dr. Orlando Costas of Costa Rica, Dr. Festo Kivengere of Uganda, and Dr. Jonathan Chao of Hong Kong. The program director in Thailand was Dr. Saphir Athyal of India. The keynote message was given by the executive secretary for the Lausanne Committee for World Evangelization, Gottfried Osei-Mensah of Ghana. In the plenary sessions there was no evidence of the ascendency of the West, and the participants seemed to feel that they all had an equal voice and

opportunity to give full expression to their views and convictions.

The COWE consultation, which convened for twelve days, was divided into seventeen mini-consultations, each of which studied the challenges and opportunities in order to produce reports and recommendations on how to reach various segments of the world's people, such as those on reaching Hindus, Muslims, Chinese, etc.

About fifty participated in the mini-consultation on reaching Chinese. The group was made up of approximately eleven "Western Christian leaders," and the rest were Chinese from Hong Kong, Taiwan, Malaysia, Singapore, the Philippines, and other Chinese groups. The chairman of the mini-consultation was Dr. Thomas Wang, a key figure in the Chinese Coordinating Office for World Evangelization (CCOWE) in Hong Kong.

The consultation on Hinduism was led by leaders from India, and so the structure of the study lent itself to the full participation and input from those who knew best about their people, their cultures, and the challenge of seeking to evangelize them. This development was most encouraging since one of the great gains for Westerners was in learning better how to listen with respect to those of other cultures.

Men and women in these relatively new positions as Christian statesmen need resources for travel and communications, as Western leaders do. Frequently, however, these Third World leaders have embarrassingly little funds available to them.

One of the great leaders of the Indian church was invited to participate in a conference in the United States—"all expenses paid." But since he was allowed to take only ten dollars in cash out of India, he arrived in this country without enough funds even to pay for phone calls. He could not extend his trip to keep an appointment in another city in the United States because he had no resources. This kind of financial embarrassment is particularly acute when a national mingles and works with affluent Western Christian leaders, who simply pull out their credit card when a need arises.

While it is false to assume that the church in the Third World is small and immature because it has no roots or strong leadership, it is also necessary to remind ourselves that the same Holy Spirit is at work in the church there as it is in the West. Just as we can misuse or foolishly handle funds God entrusts to us at times, so it is possible for a church or ministry in a developing country to do so.

But it is also true that non-Western leaders know the value of money—after all they have generally had little enough of it—and they know the needs of their people better than we do. As children of God they can be trusted to listen to His counsel, to employ honest methods, and to spend wisely—just as we trust our own leaders in the local church. This does not mean that the receiving group is not accountable for its expenditures (even Paul was eager to give careful accounts of the funds entrusted to him for the saints in Jerusalem), but we should trust nationals to make wise decisions of how to spend the money they are given.

True or False: A Missionary is Necessarily a Westerner

There are in the Third World some thirteen thousand known cross-cultural missionaries serving under non-Western agencies, funded and administered largely by their own people.

For the purposes of this book a missionary is one who takes the gospel to people who differ in at least one aspect, such as language, nationality, race or tribe from his or her own ethnic group.

Based on this definition, there are literally thousands more national Christians who are "missionaries" serving with their own church or para-church groups across cultural boundaries.

For example, Chinese churches in Singapore have taken a great interest not only in Chinese refugees in northern Thailand, but also in the unreached Yeo tribal people in that area. They are helping support several Chinese pastors and Bible teachers who minister among the Chinese and the newly opened Yeo villages. Most recently they began assisting a Chinese Bible translator in planting a church in a Lisu village in northern Thailand. Most of the half million Lisus live in China, but more than twelve thousand have spilled over into Thailand, where they have been basically unreached by the gospel.

On the other hand, when a former Brahmin priest crosses the subtle caste lines of India and serves among low caste peoples, he is working cross-culturally and should be recognized as a "missionary."

These cross-cultural missionaries often cannot take their families and minister as they feel God has called them without the material resources which Western Christians can provide.

True or False: All the Good Ideas Come from the West

Not only is it a common misconception that a missionary is necessarily a Westerner, but frequently we have the attitude that the West is "the great divide" as far as culture and ideas go, and everything is "downhill from here."

Our pride of race and culture has resulted in a paternalistic attitude which frequently does not allow us to recognize the tremendous contributions of others, both in society and in the church.

This spirit of pride manifested itself in many subtle but real ways as the modern missionary movement developed.

The history of missions in China casts light on this problem. Dedicated servants from the so-called enlightened West set sail for the "backward, benighted land of China."

In making their preparations for going, there were no cross-cultural studies or training. The ancient and highly developed culture of China, with its refinements in art, invention and philosophy, was looked upon as something to be dismantled and changed. Great accomplishments were all but ignored or held in suspicion.

As missionaries packed their steamer trunks, they might have been heard to say, "Handle the 'china' carefully, for we won't be able to get anything as nice as this over there for entertaining our important guests," forgetting that the Chinese had invented porcelain and were eating off it while most Europeans were still roaming the forests as primitive tribes.

Thus Western religion was offered but never became an integral part of China. In fact, Christianity generally became synonymous with the West's condescension. A strong yearning to be free from such Western patronage and disdain contributed to the desire of China's political leaders to find an answer for China. The Russian revolution sparked hope, and a young leader from the hinterland of China emerged—Mao Tse-tung. Mao led the communist forces to victory in 1949 and declared, "Our nation will never again be an insulted nation."

Not only do many Third World nations have a rich cultural heritage from which the West could learn much, but Christian leaders in developing countries have been saying for some time, "Let us express the gospel in ways best suited to our culture; we are mature enough to decide what is best for our church whether it be the form of worship, church government, or music."

Working with African people, one cannot help but be impressed with the ability to find happiness and meaning in life in spite of very adverse political and economic conditions.

Every tribe has a rich heritage of proverbs whose wisdom is passed on from family to family, and whose truths often have meaningful applications to the life of the Christian. For example, the East African proverb, "When elephants fight, the grass gets hurt"—explains the feelings of the powerlessness in the midst of larger conflicting forces; or "A visitor is a guest for two days—on the third day give the person a hoe"—is an African explanation of communal responsibility (or church involvement?).

The Korean church is the fastest growing church in the world and is now considering sending ten thousand cross-cultural missionaries before the end of this decade. For work within their own country Koreans already have a strong corps of leaders and much that the Western church could learn. Consider this parable, told by a Korean pastor, Lee Chang Mon, which so poignantly describes the need for cooperation in the church:

In the village of Chia Lee in Korea lived a not-too-rich young man who was about to be married. On the day before his wedding, his uncle sent him money for a new suit. With great joy he hurried off to the department store in the big city. He selected a suit, tried on the coat (which fit very well), but he did not try on the pants until he reached home late that night. Then to his deep disappointment he discovered that the pants were three inches too long. Since the wedding was to be held the following morning, there seemed to be nothing to do but to wear the pants with the legs rolled up.

The young man had a very kind grandmother who lived with them in the home. Late that night she rolled and tossed as she thought about her grandson, and the humiliation of having to wear a suit with the pants rolled up. She finally arose from her bed, slipped quietly into the room where the young man had hung his suit. She carefully took the pants from the hanger and with her big scissors she snipped off the extra three inches. She got out her needle and thread and carefully hemmed up the pants and neatly hung them in the closet. Then she went back to bed and slept in peace.

The mother of the young man had a terrible nightmare that night about her son standing before all those people with his pants rolled up, and so about two in the morning she could endure it no longer. She arose from her bed and went on tiptoe into the room where the suit was hanging. She measured carefully from the bottom of the pants and with her scissors snipped off the pants and then hemmed neatly and completely.

Very early the next morning before the sun had begun to rise the older sister of the young lad arose from her bed. Hers had been a troubled night of sleep. Before anyone else was up, she slipped quietly into his room and removed his suit from the hanger. Using her scissors expertly she removed three inches from the bottom of the pants, hemmed them carefully and put them back on the hanger.

You can well imagine the consternation of the young man as he pulled on his trousers later that morning just before the wedding. They barely covered his knees.

The point is clear. There was a great lack in communication and cooperation. Even though each of the three ladies intended well and even finished the job with a feeling of accomplishment, the end result was tragic.

This is oriental humor with a pungency none too relishing. It highlights our failure to function as one body. We forget when the members of our body do not work harmoniously and cooperatively, we are prone to become sick, handicapped and even dead.[6]

Not only does the Third World church have meaningful ways of teaching truth at the grassroots level, but its leadership is putting out a growing number of well-documented and thought-provoking books that speak to the whole question of the church and missions: e.g., *The Church and Its Mission, A Shattering Critique From the Third World,* by Orlando Costas of Costa Rica; or *Independence for the Third World Churches*, by Pius Wakatama of Zimbabwe.

No, all the good ideas do not come necessarily from the West. Gordon MacDonald, author and pastor, reinforces this view:

> My own estimation is that some of the greatest preaching in the world is being done today by Africans, Asians and Latins. God is raising up people who in their own culture are far more effective than anybody here. And we've got to deal with that.
>
> We used to assume that they'd get all the energy, all the wisdom, all the resources from here. And that's not true anymore . . . the rest of the world has an awful lot to give us.[7]

Yes, we must rid ourselves of the misconceptions that:
—nationals will be spoiled if we help them
—we cannot help an indigenous ministry
—we can't trust "younger" churches with money
—a missionary is necessarily a Westerner
—all the good ideas come from the West.

If we can do this, then it will be easy to accept the fact that assisting nationals makes good sense.

Notes

1. Roger E. Coon, "Unchanging Task: Changing Roles," *Evangelical Missions Quarterly*, Vol. 16, No. 4, October 1980, p. 208.
2. T. Stanley Soltau, *Missions at the Crossroads*, Van Kampen Press, Wheaton, IL, 1954, p. 117.
3. Pius Wakatama, *Independence for the Third World Church, An African's Perspective on Missionary Work*, Inter-Varsity Press, Downer's Grove, IL, 1976, p. 37.
4. Herbert Kane, *A Global View of Christian Missions*, Baker Book House, Grand Rapids, Michigan, 1971, page 14.
5. C. Peter Wagner, *Stop the World, I Want To Get On*, Regal Books, Glendale, CA, 1974, pp. 102-103.
6. D. John Richard, "Evangelical Cooperation," *AIM*, November, 1980, pp. 6,7.
7. Gordon MacDonald, "Your Church in God's Global Plan," *Chrisitan Herald*, November, 1980, p. 49.

5

ASSISTING NATIONALS
MAKES GOOD SENSE

Now that we've cleared away some of the misconceptions about supporting nationals, let's consider the logical reasons why supporting them is a feasible way to relieve the energy crisis in missions.

1. *In many developing countries there is a corps of trained and dedicated national leaders who are ready to step out into service for God.*

In the world of evangelists, Argentinian Luis Palau has become almost as well known as Billy Graham. His team has held highly visible and successful campaigns throughout Central and South America, across the United States and even in Europe. More than two hundred thousand people attended his meetings in Scotland, and thousands made Christian commitments. Palau, equally at home with English as with his native Spanish, is a forceful evangelist and Bible expositor and is highly respected. He is frequently called upon as a speaker at international congresses and conferences.

But for every national leader of Palau's world status, there are hundreds of gifted, committed Christian leaders who are ready and willing to serve Christ among their own people.

For example, when Evangelista Siodora took over the leadership of the Philippine Missionary Fellowship in 1978, there were forty missionaries and thirty-five trained Bible school students who had applied to become missionaries under PMF. These young people were eager to serve in the rural areas of the Philippines even though they knew they would earn only a few dollars a month. Three years later there were ninety-five missionaries and another forty-six candidates waiting to be accepted as soon as the Lord provided the funds.

In Indonesia, when Dr. Chris Marantika began a church planting ministry, he let it be known that he needed trained and experienced church planters. Within a few months he had eleven men, all with some Bible training, and several with seminary degrees, who were willing to join him to start churches in Muslim areas where there was no other gospel witness.

From India *Christian Nationals* received more than seventy applications in one year from ministries who needed help to expand. Trained personnel were available, but funds were not. Donald McGavran believes the enormous reservoir of potential missionaries in the nineteen million professing Christians of that country lies largely untapped.

Though leadership is lacking in some areas (e.g., Africa, where the church is fast outgrowing its trained leadership), many parts of the Third World are reaping the harvest of the education programs established by Western missions.

The World Directory of Mission-Related Education Institutions lists more than six hundred theological schools of all levels and doctrinal positions in the Third World. Many of these do not require more than a primary education for entrance and may offer only one or two years of training. But some missiologists estimate that the level of mission Bible school training offered is sufficient for ninety percent of the work needed. It is not too academic or disoriented from village life, and evangelists and pastors can readily fit back into the culture from which they came. In addition to the students in resident schools, thousands of local leaders around the world are being trained through Theological Education by Extension (TEE) programs.

In Asia alone eighty theological schools are registered with the evangelically-oriented Asia Theological Association.

There has been wasted effort, of course: duplication (in some cities a dozen small theological schools may compete for students), and institutions built to satisfy the ego of the persons founding them—but generally the schools have produced a qualified corps of Christian leaders in the developing countries.

There has, however, been a drastic shortage of higher level theological education to train the professors, scholars, and writers of the Third World. For example, there is only one evangelical graduate level seminary for all of French-speaking Africa. The newly opened Nairobi Evangelical Graduate School of Theology is the first graduate level English-medium seminary on the continent.

Thus a flood of students has poured into seminaries and Christian graduate schools in the West, often with devastating results. Dr. Bong Rin Ro, general secretary of the Asia Theological Association, estimates that ninety-five percent of all students (both Christian and secular) who left Taiwan to study abroad in the past twenty years never returned to Taiwan.

The church has not only lost much of its potential leadership through the "brain drain," but also to secular employment because all too often the church does not have jobs available for Bible school graduates.

Not only is there a shortage of jobs related to the church that offer a "living" wage, but governments in newly established countries, especially in Africa, are desperate for well-trained leadership. In one African country a leader who returned home after earning his M.R.E. in the United States was approached by officials who pled with him to serve as vice president of the country. Another young man who returned home after his college training in North America was approached to serve as minister of education of a new African republic. Praise God both of these men had firmly established their priorities years before and are still in full-time Christian work today.

2. *The church in the Third World does not have enough financial resources to evangelize, train, and disciple the unreached masses.*

The sacrifice made by men with such qualifications can only be appreciated when one understands the economies of many developing countries. For example, while the 1980 per capita gross national product in the United States was $9700 per year, in Africa it was only $530, yet inflation rises faster in many Third World countries than in the West. In Ghana, for example, in 1983 an egg cost a day's wages, and in Argentina inflation rose to an annual rate of four hundred percent.

Thus Christian workers in these areas often find it difficult to provide even the barest of essentials for their families.

Kenyan missionaries living on the coastal plains are miles from a source of water during the dry season. They do have corrugated iron roofs on their homes and could collect rain water in tanks during the rainy season, but the tanks cost about one hundred dollars a piece, and they don't have the money to buy them.

A chaplain in the hospitals in Kinshasa, Zaire, weeps over the patients he ministers to because they are hungry. Custom here dictates that family members must provide daily food, but when patients come in from the country for urgent treatment, they may not have anyone to cook for them. The chaplains would like to help, but their meager allowances make it impossible for them to do so.

A Filipino missionary may have his housing supplied by the village people, but he must purchase his own food. Siodora says they often live on "native potatoes" twice a day for weeks on end.

In the urban areas where there are better paying jobs, Christian workers do receive better wages, but traditionally the extended family expects to share in the largess, and anyone unwilling to do so would be considered stingy and egotistical and be a poor Christian testimony. It is not unusual for a pastor's family to include half a dozen nieces and nephews, aged parents, an aunt and uncle or two, and even a country cousin. "Caring for" includes providing education for the children.

Added to the economic difficulties of national workers is the fact that the numerical base from which their support should come is very small in relation to the population. Figure 1 indicates the percentage of evangelical Christians in the major areas of the world. Even France, which has enjoyed a highly developed civilization for centuries, has only sixty thousand evangelical believers out of a population of fifty-two million (one tenth of one percent). It stands to reason that it would be difficult for this small minority to adequately finance the evangelism, teaching and discipling ministry that is needed to build the church in France. Yet there is a growing corps of young people coming out of European Bible schools each year who would like nothing more than to put their total time and effort into doing just that.

Figure 1 Percentages of Evangelical Christians

Western World	**13.0**
Africa	**8.0**

Latin America	**6.0**
Communist Bloc	**1.1**
Asia	**1.1**
The Pacific	**17.0**
The Caribbean	**6.0**
The Middle East	**0.2**

From *Operation World* by P.J. Johnstone

Therefore, from the standpoint of the economic need alone, it makes good sense to support national workers until their own church or economy is able to take over.

3. *It makes good sense to support nationals because they know the language and culture (or near culture) so that they can easily adapt themselves to the lifestyle of the people with whom they work.*

Communications principles teach that the more alike the communicator and the person to whom he is communicating are, the more readily the communicator will be understood.

It takes a foreign missionary several years to become fluent in the national language. Unfortunately most missionaries never learn the language well enough to communicate on an intimate level with the people.

Yet nationals frequently are able to speak several major languages from their background and education. It is not uncommon, for example, for young people in Soweto, the African township outside of Johannesburg, to speak both the official languages of South Africa (English and Afrikaans) as well as five or six Bantu languages. These are distinct tribal languages, but have some basic similarities in vocabulary and structure. With such a background, the acquisition of other languages becomes an exciting challenge—almost a hobby—and these Africans can quickly pick up another tribal language when needed.

While it may take a foreign missionary several years to learn a language well enough to use it, he or she may never understand the "deep secrets" of the culture—the significance of certain customs and traditions and the subtle innuendos of personal relationships and tribal hierarchy.

They may think that they understand the natives, but they know they can seldom live just as they do. Sanitation, health hazards, diet, social customs, lack of privacy, excessive heat, insects, lack of medical facilities, and substandard schools may all be part of the lifestyle, particularly in the rural areas of developing countries. As one national leader has expressed it, "Some very spiritual and dedicated Western missionaries have tried to live in the villages just like our national missionaries. But most can't do it; they end up broken in health. We find very few couples with families can live for very long in the manner of primitive people."

Of course it must be admitted that there are "prejudice" barriers (especially between some tribal groups) that often prevent neighbors from working in another group.

But generally nationals who have come from backgrounds similar to the people whom they are reaching can adjust more readily.

For example, Jacob and Rosie Devasagayam are both medical doctors. After completing their training in India they came to the United States for specialist training—he in surgery and she in gynecology. The lure of a "double" medical practice in the West was strong, but God gave them no peace until they returned to India to work among poor village people who had no other medical care.

They decided to live in a village themselves, in a mud house with no running water or telephone, and "bare bulb" electricity. Rosie says, "We became like one of the villagers—we understood them, and they understood us."

After four years the Devasagayams moved into a larger

town where they opened a small clinic from which they traveled together by scooter to hold roadside clinics in the villages.

Jacob and Rosie can do this. As Indians, they speak the language fluently; they understand the taboos and customs of the villagers; they are accustomed to the food; they are comfortable living a lifestyle that would test most Westerners to the limit.

The Devasagayams illustrate one of the basic advantages national leaders have—the nationals know the language and culture, and can easily adapt themselves to the lifestyle of those with whom they work.

4. *Supporting nationals makes good sense because they can continue to build the church in countries where doors have been closed to traditional missions.*

With almost forty nations refusing or greatly restricting visas for foreign missionaries, it obviously makes good sense to help the national Christians within those countries take the best advantage possible of their opportunities.

In Bangladesh, for example, certain tribal areas are closed even to tourists because the political situation is potentially explosive. Yet citizens of Bangladesh can get permission to move into these areas freely. Subhas Sangma, formerly executive secretary of the Evangelical Fellowship of Bangladesh, now heads a group of church planters and evangelists who are entering these areas. To help them in this important task is not only logical, but also essential since there is no one else with the vision or the opportunity to do so.

Burma is another country closed to foreign mission work. When all missionaries were put out of the country in 1966, a small virile church was left behind, but there were still many areas where the gospel had never penetrated.

The Burmese church has experienced rapid growth and

revival in recent years. For example, a team of thirteen itinerant evangelists visited unreached villages. Within a short time they had baptized two thousand believers and formed thirteen congregations. Christians in Singapore began hearing these reports when a few of the converts came to a small Bible school on the Thai-Burma border, which was being assisted by Singapore churches.

These dedicated young evangelists traveled for months on end without any promise of regular support. They started out from their home village with just enough money to get to the next village, depending on the kindness of the local people to put them up—a practice used by Buddhist monks as they wander through the countryside. When the evangelists completed their meetings, they took an offering that supported their needs until they reached the next place.

The team even traveled into China and Laos, bringing back stories of miraculous conversions, release from demons, and whole villages turning to Christ—villages that had never once "since creation" (according to one evangelist) heard the name of Christ.

There was just one problem—some of these young men had families back home who were existing with very little support from them. Christians in Singapore and friends of *Christian Nationals* in the West began helping ease the load and had the blessed privilege of sharing in these "acts of the apostles in Burma."

This team reinforces the idea that national Christian leaders can often build the church in areas where doors have been closed to traditional missions.

5. *Not only can outside assistance help launch an effective national ministry, but assistance, wisely given, can serve as a catalyst for local support.*

Probably the most familiar way to stimulate such reciprocal giving is the "matching grant," though this may not always be the right approach since there may not be a church large enough or no church at all to "match."

One large European foundation takes this into account in its grant program and will offer two-thirds or even three-quarters of the needed funds, requiring the national church to raise the balance within the country or through other friends.

But sometimes just the promise of funds is enough to stir up "possibility thinking" among people who usually dare not think big, because nothing ever comes of their dreams. Thus there is the tendency to plan small advances, inadequate buildings, and to be satisfied with too few or untrained personnel because that's all they ever had.

Just to see hope given wings through a promise of needed funds for a project can sometimes lift the whole program to a new perspective.

For example, Nigerian evangelist Moses Ariye decided to leave the pastorate of a large church to lead a countrywide evangelistic program in many denominations, both in city campaigns and university towns. He and his family of six children lived in a tiny corrugated iron house and tried to carry on the administration of the growing *Gospel Light Ministry* out of their home.

Thousands were flocking to hear this dynamic African preacher, but he was hampered on every side by lack of funds for literature, travel, co-workers' salaries, preparations, and follow-up. He needed office space, housing for staff, a place to train leaders, etc.

His board approached *Christian Nationals,* who agreed to help build a headquarters and accommodations for the Ariye family.

By the time the first installment of the pledged amount arrived, Moses wrote back to thank the donors and said,

"You won't need to send any more money. When the local people saw the foundation going in and the building starting to go up, they began to contribute, and we have enough money on hand to complete it. Your help was all they needed to give them hope that this project could become a reality."

On numerous occasions the "seed" money for a project has been enough of a catalyst to stimulate local giving to meet the need.

6. *Supporting nationals makes good sense because leaders in top echelons of church leadership often need outside assistance until the church is educated and able to carry the program on its own.*

The evangelical church in the Third World has become more visible and influential as it has closed ranks and strengthened its ties locally and internationally.

Small congregations need the advantage of seminars and TEE training for their leadership provided for them. Young people need the reinforcement of being part of a larger body, such as an inter-church fellowship. Educational facilities cannot be operated without a broad base of support. The church needs to come to grips with the problems in society, speak out against injustice, take a stand against doctrinal erosion. To do this it needs strong, visible leadership.

But a small congregation whose members are living on subsistence farming or very little cash income can barely care for their own church, and have neither the funds nor the vision to support church executives or denominational programs. In fact, the vast majority of churches in the Third World do not have full-time pastors supported by the local church.

One can then understand why these churches cannot and do not contribute very much to the top denominational or church leadership that is so vital to the internal as well as numerical growth of the church.

Thus these men become "squeezed out at the top" without an adequate support base when they leave the fairly secure positions in the large local churches that have been able to support a full-time pastor. They represent the national church, and are not subordinate or responsible to foreign mission bodies. They are well-educated men who need to travel within the country as well as to have contact with the church in other parts of the world. But they have extremely limited resources to draw upon until the local church becomes able and educated to the necessity of assisting such leaders of denominational or evangelical fellowships.

It makes good sense to assist men like Isaac Simbiri, executive secretary of the Evangelical Fellowship of Kenya. Simbiri is a gifted Bible teacher and Christian educator. He left a vital position in the Christian education department of the Africa Inland Church to accept the offer to lead EFK, whose primary goal is to provide training and materials for Kenya's fast-growing church. When Simbiri joined EFK, there were funds on hand for exactly one month's salary and a praying committee who promised to present the needs as they could.

With *Christian Nationals'* assistance during the first few crucial years, EFK has time to educate and inform the churches of Kenya of its ministry and to develop a support base within the country.

EFK is just one illustration of why it makes good sense to assist the top leadership in national churches.

7. *Assisting national leaders makes good sense because they can more closely model a Christian family within the context of the culture.*

For years a Western missionary couple had helped run

camps for African young people, often spending precious school holiday time cooking and chauffeuring for African youngsters so they could have a special camping experience. The young people observed their dedication and selfless service.

But when they saw an African couple doing the same, the impact was greater. At one girls' retreat, where the African woman leader was speaking as well as cooking for the girls, two of the campers were overheard saying, "Just look, Sis May can serve the Lord like that because Jerry is willing to stay home and take care of children." That willingness was certainly cutting across traditional cultural practices, but it made an impression on Christian young people observing it. Hundreds of Christian young people have testified that Jerry and May set a standard for marriage and family life that they hoped to emulate.

Christian families are on the defensive the world over—but the enemy's tactics are different in each culture. Only someone "inside" the culture can really fully demonstrate God's grace for the testings.

For example, the Kavalukus, Kenyan missionaries who work among the Giriama tribe, had a difficult test to pass.

Their baby died! A little sister for her two brothers, she'd been long awaited. But among the Giriamas in Kenya there's only the old midwife, with her years of experience in the customs of the tribe, to help the young mother—and all too often that help isn't enough.

But strangely, Anna Kavaluku was not bitter about the loss of her child. In fact, she thanked the old granny over and over for her solicitous care. And the other women in the village, dressed in their tattered dirty skirts, an end of which was pulled over their sagging bosoms to show their respect to her, came with offerings of food, or simply to sit with her in her sorrow.

The baby died. But the village opened its heart to the missionary and his wife in their loss. Somehow they seemed one of them now, this strange Kamba couple who had come from the highlands of Kenya to live among them.

For four years they had shared the same simple fare, living on the edge of the village in the same kind of mud and grass house, walking two miles to the nearest river for water. The village is rightly named "Shauri Mowra" (Place of Sorrow) because there is no water nearby.

The village gods had lost their power anyway ("See," the old men laugh, "even their house has fallen down"), so perhaps the new God that Jonah and Anna talked about was more powerful. They responded slowly and cautiously—after all the Giriamas resisted change for centuries—but they are listening now. Many began coming to the little mud church Jonah built near his house.

"Look," they are saying to each other, "Anna's God has sent a new little one who is healthy and strong. Perhaps this God will help our village too."

Anna and Jonah Kavaluku just keep on loving, teaching, and modeling, trusting that one day these Giriama villagers will fully commit themselves to the God who has answered their prayer.

The Kavalukus demonstrated that they could face the same trials under the same conditions as the villagers, and prove Christ sufficient.

8. *Supporting nationals to relieve the energy crisis in missions makes good sense because you can get a lot of mileage out of your money.*

To some this may sound brazen or manipulative, but it would be helpful if you recall a basic principle usually followed in establishing a Christian worker's salary:

He or she should be able to live at the standard of those to whom he or she is ministering. Many churches in the

West determine the pastor's salary, at least partially, on the average income of his parishioners. He should not live so high above those to whom he is ministering that his lifestyle causes jealousy or resentment, or that he cannot relate to the problems and needs of his people. He should be able to demonstrate a sensitivity to the needs of the poor and be able to teach stewardship without hypocrisy.

On the other hand, those who support him should be able to respect him and should follow the biblical injunction that "the laborer is worthy of his hire."

One of the difficulties encountered by Western missionaries is that in many cases their lifestyle and salary scale have placed them far above the people with whom they work. You don't have to talk with national Christians very long to realize that this has been a source of tension, jealousy and resentment. National missionaries, of course, are not immune to the desire for material goods and security and can easily fall into the same trap.

However, if the local board of the national leader determines the salary scale, it will generally be realistic about what the worker needs to care adequately for his family and to do his work efficiently, what the people in the area are earning, and what would be an equitable allowance.

Here are some average allowances set by local boards in developing countries for various categories of ministry in 1983. The wide divergence in monthly salary is due to the local conditions and inflation:

Country	Position	Average monthly allowance (in U.S. dollars)
Argentina	urban evangelist	$1,050
Bangladesh	rural church planter	$55–110
India	trained nurse in village	$80
India	village evangelist	$35–85

Indonesia	pastor (rural)	$80–150
Kenya	urban worker	$600–1,200
Korea	church planter	$120–300
Singapore	pastor	$800–1,200
South Africa	urban worker	$600–1,000

Contrast this with the average monthly support required for a Western missionary and family, which is twenty-five hundred to three thousand dollars. It should also be noted that very few of these workers need furlough funds, medical insurance (most countries provide available medical services at very low cost), boarding schools for children, etc.

On the other hand, the cost of living in many Third World countries is escalating rapidly, and it should not be expected that these low pay scales should or will continue. However, with earning power increasing in the churches, more of the costs are being shared by the local bodies.

Yes, supporting nationals is a logical way to help ease the energy crisis in missions, but it could not have been possible without the dedication and sacrifice of Western missionaries, particularly in the great missionary program of this century. The lasting effectiveness of the movement was demonstrated where persecution or war left the national church standing on its own as happened in China.

Furthermore, assisting nationals is not without its problems. Any church or individual embarking on such a program would do well to be aware of the dangers and disappointments inherent in it.

It takes an organization of considerable experience to avoid competing with local sources of funds, for example. This is not a case for amateurism. Let's look at some problems.

6

LET'S FACE THE PROBLEMS

It is possible to be of assistance to the younger churches without being paternalistic. I do believe that we owe them more than manpower or wisdom or history. . . . We do have an obligation to our sister churches because God has so richly and so bountifully blessed us. Admittedly, this is one of the precarious matters . . . how can we do this without permitting to rise within ourselves a feeling of paternalism, consciously or unconsciously? At the same time, how can we do this so that the recipient will not feel an over-indebtedness to us and become bound and his freedom become limited, or that he develops a feeling of dependence upon us, or that our assistance becomes a stifling factor in their sense of sacrifice and their sense of responsibility?[1]

Let's face it—assisting nationals is not without its problems and frustrations. If we are not aware of this possibility, we may become easily disillusioned at the first disappointment. National Christian leaders are not more supernatural, or less human than we are.

For example, Reverend X was the head of a large overseas denomination. His qualities of leadership and influence took him to the top; but the church was not able to pay for the expenses of travel, administration and facilities commensurate with his responsibilities. The board of the independent church asked for assistance from a Western mission organization, and this help was given for a number of years before it was discovered that funds had been siphoned off for Reverend X's own personal family needs—an elaborate

90

home (by national standards) and a car kept in his own name and used for a family business.

Though misuse of funds like this rarely happens, there are other problems that frequently arise to cause misunderstanding and bring about unrealistic expectations. Being aware of these possible difficulties will help us avoid them, or recognize them for what they are.

Selection Process Can Be Faulty

Though we will be discussing how to select national projects wisely in a later chapter, it is important to note this is one of the basic problems.

The world is growing smaller, and today hundreds of people go abroad for conferences, serve short-term missionary assignments or visit mission fields as "Christian tourists."

Even though their short tours may give them superficial impressions and understanding of the situation, these Christian travelers may bring back all kinds of projects and needs. Frequently they encourage their churches to become involved financially, or they may do so individually. Sometimes they will donate the first five hundred dollars on the spot, and then find themselves facing the problem of raising the balance of a fifty thousand dollar project when they return home.

Pastors from North American churches are increasingly going on overseas tours, often without much background in mission administration or orientation to the pitfalls of becoming involved in giving assistance to nationals.

One pastor, for example, was greatly impressed by the man who served as his interpreter and made a promise to "see what he could do to help his ministry get moving." He found out that such casual words of encouragement were taken almost as a solemn promise of assistance, and have resulted in misunderstanding and hurt feelings.

Another pastor visited a ministry led by a national, and likewise became involved to the extent that he now feels obligated to invite this leader to the church's missionary conference. This commits the church to considerable travel expense and an almost built-in obligation to become directly involved in his ministry. Meanwhile, after further investigation, the church's missionary committee has decided this is not the type of program in which they want their church to become involved.

On the other hand, many bright prospective leaders are coming to study in the West. Frequently they attend local churches and meet individuals who influence or support their desire to start some new and independent project with the promise of backing from North America. This may cause a key leader to remove himself from the accountability to his own national church and the influence of wise and established local leaders while he seeks independently to further his own vision. Sometimes Westerners without mission experience will even offer to form a "board" and incorporate the new ministry in the West so as to qualify for tax-exempt status.

Not only does this weaken the leadership of the local church, but it removes the national leader from the guidance, correction and strengths of the national body, and encourages him to satisfy those who "pay the piper."

Domination Through Money

Unless very careful guidelines are followed, the adage "he who pays the piper calls the tune" becomes true. Money can be a subtle form of persuasion and influence, and unless funding can be "neutralized" in some way, the receiving body will continue to conform to expectations in order to maintain the funding. This can hinder independence and authentic growth.

It is all too easy to adopt church worship forms, leadership roles, associations and expression of theology to conform unnecessarily with a Western pattern when there is the fear that change might result in loss of revenue.

How to avoid this hidden pressure is a very real problem to any Western body contributing funds to a national ministry, particularly when the Western donors do not understand the culture in which the national ministry is growing.

Cultural Differences Cause Differences in Expectations

When a Western church or para-church organization assists a national ministry, there are usually certain basic expectations:

Regular reporting

Audited accounting and honoring "designated funds" religiously

Goals and objectives related to time

Clear organizational structure and accountability

Open communication—everything "up front"

In a missionary scenario, Dennis Clark sums up our expectations in a fictitious discussion between mission executives concerning turning funds over to the national church.

"But what about the money, fellows? It's our money. They want to control our money!" a voice said from the end of the table.

"Is it our money? Where did it come from?" Bob Johnson rapped the table.

"Well, sure. The churches, the individual supporters gave to OUR mission."

"Did they really give it to us or to God?" Ted Hill broke in.

93

"Look, let's get this straight. When money is given to God it is neutralized. Why shouldn't the Asian teams be just as good trustees as ourselves? YOU ARE TALKING LIKE A BUSINESS MAN, not as a servant of God."[2]

Business expectations—that's the way we operate our churches and missions in the West, and that's the way we expect Third World ministries to operate. And when they don't, there are misunderstandings.

For example, American donors want to hear regular reports from those whom they support. But when one visits the field and sees the circumstances under which nationals frequently have to work, it is easy to understand why reports are not readily forthcoming. Transportation is not only expensive but irregular and often nonexistent. When Evangelista Siodora visits the missionaries of the PMF to encourage and help them (and incidentally to monitor their work), he may travel by boat, jeep, and bus for several days, and end up climbing a mountain by foot for hours before reaching his destination.

When Paul Chang visits the refugee villages in northern Thailand, it involves an expensive flight and a dusty truck ride up a dangerous one-lane dirt road before reaching a mountaintop village.

Reports made by workers on the field may be written in Chinese, Telegu, Tagalog, etc.—they must be translated into English before being sent to their sponsors in the West.

Postal services are frequently irregular or nonexistent. Letters from isolated parts of some countries may take months to get to their destination—or they may never arrive at all.

Not only may reports be time-consuming and difficult to obtain, but the Western practice of exposing our feelings is not typical in most Third World cultures. On the other hand, some Asians follow cultural patterns and feel they should belittle themselves and not seem boastful to give positive reports. The Chinese have a gracious practice of "saving face," which sometimes keeps the negative aspects hidden. Some African tribes believe it is polite and respectful to "tell the hearer what he wants to hear" rather than to hurt him with distressing facts. In Korea to ask someone to be more specific could be taken as disrespect.

It took Western missionaries many years to accept that these practices were not deceitful, but cultural patterns that had to be understood. How then can Westerners who have never lived in another culture understand the problems of objective reporting from a Third World ministry?

If expecting regular and objective reporting causes problems, requiring balanced and audited accounting can be even more fraught with difficulty.

One African worker who headed a large and very effective ministry in central Africa complained, "Why should Africans report on the way they spend the money when missionaries never reported to Africans?" He went on to explain that the concept of reporting to someone who gives you a gift is alien to their culture.

In the patterns of the extended family in many countries it becomes very difficult to say "no" to a need in the family if there is money on hand from any source. When Southern Baptist missionary John Carpenter was assigned to work in Liberia with an old black missionary from Texas, Mother George, she referred to him jokingly as "the great white elephant." But for the first time in almost fifty years of her work in Africa she could send people to someone else when they came for help. Carpenter admits that Mother George was good-hearted. "She just didn't realize that people were taking advantage of her. . . . I put her on a budget and made available only a certain amount of money to be spent on materials, etc. When her helpers came down to get supplies, for the first time in her years in Africa she was able to operate in the black, and that was simply because I defended her from those who would take advantage of her."[3]

Even this daughter of slaves from the American South could not say no to her "family" when a need was expressed. (How Scriptural can you be?) Harold Fuller describes this holistic use of money and possessions:

In nonindustrialized cultures money and possessions are looked at very holistically. Produce belongs to a community; the extended family shares with its members according to need not individual ownership. When a holistic-oriented person takes a job in an office where money is strictly accounted for, he often gets into trouble. He 'borrows' money from the cash box to meet an urgent need; the money is not being used, and he will replace it before it is needed, he reasons. However, his holistic optimism over replacing it does not materialize in reality, and he finds himself unaccountably charged with embezzlement![4]

Third World leaders themselves will be the first to admit that this philosophy has to change and, in fact, has already undergone rapid change. But there is a great need to train bookkeepers and accountants for churches in the Third World so that their desire to keep records and make financial reports can be matched by their ability to do so. Even then it must be accepted that entries may reflect their own style which might not be clear to a Western accountant.

However, Gordon MacDonald warns of the danger of our expectations: "It is the North American mind-set always to think in terms of accountability. Accountability is a great managerial technique and expectation." He goes on to explain that he believes the mature church overseas does not mind accounting for *how* it spends the money of Christians, but that the church should not be expected to make its investments according to American priorities or interests.[5]

When it comes to time orientation, the West has no equal. Thus when churches send questonnaires to evaluate their national ministries, they want to know, "How many hours a week do you spend in ministry?" or "Give a report of a typical day" (meaning "How do you spend your time?"). Goals and objectives have become the supreme test of the effectiveness and worth of a ministry—and nationals are asked to outline their short-term and long-term goals in measurable, time-oriented terms.

Anthropologists have long been telling us that most Western cultures are time oriented, while many Third World cultures are event oriented. To them it is not important to start and stop a meeting on time; it is important to allow people to work over a problem or an idea until it is resolved or exhausted. People in such cultures are usually interested in the here and now, not in history.

Closely aligned to event orientation is the importance of personal interaction and developing relationships. Conversation is more important than accomplishing a task. In many cultures, group interaction and getting involved with people is more important than achieving specific goals. Great effort has been made to introduce these very perspectives into our own Western culture in recent years.

Missionaries struggled for years trying to get nationals to keep time by installing bells to call people to church and scolding those who came late. They found it difficult to understand the family that spent its month's allowance in the first few days and then struggled from hand to mouth for the rest of the month because they didn't plan ahead. They could not understand how a church leader could miss an important meeting because an old friend had dropped by for a visit. And in turn the national Christian was often puzzled when the missionary wanted to shorten the service to end at a certain time, or when he would curtail a visit in order to run off to keep an appointment.

Over the years these differences have been recognized as cultural. Today Africans will jokingly announce a meeting time adding, "And that's not African time." With the pressures of Western society invading so much of the Third World, time and goal orientation has become more natural—though not necessarily an improvement—in the culture.

Yet, not recognizing these differences can cause the donor who is looking for reports, financial statements, and organizational structures, goals, and objectives to misunderstand the effectiveness of a ministry because it does not conform to his expectation.

Problem Attitudes Can Arise

Even with the most careful selection and agreements between funding body and national ministry, problem attitudes can develop. Ted Engstrom warns that "philanthropy can often do more harm than good because it has a tendency to make the recipient feel obligated and dependent . . . it encourages inactivity and a laissez faire attitude. Perhaps that is why so many foreigners seem to dislike Americans so thoroughly. Handouts and doles can easily lead to lack of respect and dignity."[6]

National leaders are also recognizing these dangers. One Indian worker who had been involved in extensive flood relief in his area vowed never again to take charge of a relief program. He saw that the "refugee complex" too easily became a permanent attitude in the minds of the people.

Ted Ward, a leading Western educator, reinforces this reaction. "The logic of relief and the logic of development are fundamentally contradictory. Relief activity is essentially counter-developmental. Relief activity has the potential for creating an even greater development problem. . . . Relief is addictive."[7]

98

Just as it becomes difficult to wean refugees from relief, it can become difficult to wean churches and Christian ministries from assistance, if an attitude of dependence and laissez faire is allowed to develop. Some churches begun during refugee periods twenty-five years ago still expect Western aid for their pastors and programs.

Furthermore, some nationals, like some Western Christian leaders, can have unrealistic and ego-oriented expectations. Position and education can go to their heads, causing them to demand benefits so that they "live as they deserve," far above the level of the people to whom they minister. Unfortunately they see too many examples of this in the Western church to break this expectation easily.

On the other hand, many national leaders find it far easier to identify with the people in their culture than Western missionaries do. For example, an Indonesian who earned his doctorate in the United States returned to his homeland with only his barrels of books. He and his wife agreed they would take none of the Western gadgets and luxuries they had accumulated during their years in America so that they could more easily relate back to their society.

One problem attitude that may be difficult to identify, until vast sums of money have been spent, is the visionary or dreamer with creative ideas that are beyond the capabilities of his people at this point in history. Westerners are impressed with a well-thought-out project, spelled out in measurable terms with high expectations. And national leaders who have been educated in our graduate schools and seminaries and have seen effective programs in Western churches have learned to think in those terms and dream longingly of how their people could be evangelized, educated, and "lifted" through an expensive "short cut."

However, implementing the project is another thing once they arrive back in their own country, armed with equipment, programs, and funding. Suddenly they are back to the realities of heat and humidity that destroy equipment, personnel with limited training, traditional practices resistant to change, isolation from people who could help, communication problems—and the big idea fizzles.

As a result, the tendency may be to denounce the leader as dishonest or, at the least, foolish, rather than to empathize with his dreams and his frustrations and help him to face the situation in his own country realistically. We never know when that "dreamer" will be the touchstone of a whole new movement for God that revolutionizes the church in his country.

Let Them Make Their Own Mistakes

We have attempted to present the most common problems faced when assisting national leaders. Rather than becoming discouraged at this array of problems, we should remember Christ's words, "Let him who is without sin cast the first stone." No Christian organization is perfect; no leader is without faults; no program is ever completely fulfilled.

We make many mistakes; we must allow the national church to make her own, and to stand before her God, as we will, confessing, weeping, and praising Him for His mercy and grace.

We must allow the national church to make her own judgments based on culture and experience. We must allow her to express doctrine in her own frame of reference—not compromising truth, but trusting the Holy Spirit to guide her into all truth.

George Peters illustrates this in a conversation with Bakht Singh, a well-known Indian pastor:

As we talked about evangelism and a message for India, I asked him:

"When you preach in India, what do you emphasize? Do you preach to them the *love* of God?"

"No," he said, "not particularly. The Indian mind is so polluted that if you talk to them about love they think mainly of sex life. You do not talk to them much about the love of God."

"Well," I said, "do you talk to them about the *wrath* of God and the judgment of God?"

"No, this is not my emphasis," he remarked, "they are used to that. All the gods are mad anyway. It makes no difference to them if there is one more who is angry!"

"What do you talk to them about? Do you preach Christ and Him crucified?" I guessed.

"No," he replied. "They would think of Him as a poor martyr who helplessly died."

"What then is your emphasis, do you talk to them about eternal life?"

"Not so," he said, "if you talk about eternal life, the Indian thinks of transmigration. He wants to get away from it. Don't emphasize eternal life."

"What then is your message?"

"I have never yet failed to get a hearing if I talk to them about forgiveness of sins and peace and rest in your heart. That's the product that sells well. Soon they ask me how they can get it. Having won their hearing I lead them on to the Savior who alone can meet their deepest needs."

That is what we mean by *configuration of message*. Not in any way does it imply a cutting down of the gospel. It seeks to win a hearing in order to present the gospel.[8]

Dr. Peters went on to warn that to continue with this kind of lopsided approach could lead to sectarianism, but that as an "opener" it is effective within the context of India. National leaders should have the freedom to present biblical truths in a meaningful way in their own culture without condemnation from their Western co-partners.

It may seem from our discussion of problems that all the adjustment, understanding, and willingness to change must come from the Western donors if they are to become involved in assisting national ministries.

This is far from the truth. In fact, this would just further demonstrate the very paternalism we are trying to avoid. Genuine cooperation depends upon consultation and mutual reciprocity, which is the touchstone of relationships that could result in the evangelization of the world.

Notes

1. Wade Coggins, and E. L. Frizen, Jr. "Issues Confronting Evangelical Missions," *Evangelical Missions Tomorrow,* William Carey Library, Pasadena, California, 1977, p. 157.
2. Dennis Clark, *The Third World and Missions,* Word Publishers, Waco, Texas, 1971, pp. 125.
3. Lorry Lutz, *Born to Lose, Bound to Win,* Harvest House, Irvine, California, 1980, p. 176.
4. Harold Fuller, *Mission Church Dynamics,* William Carey Library, Pasadena, California, 1980, pp. 182, 183.
5. Gordon MacDonald, "Your Church in God's Global Plan," *Christian Herald,* November, 1980, p. 52.
6. Ted Engstrom, *What in the World is God Doing? The New Face of Missions,* Word Publishers, Waco, Texas, 1978, p. 101.
7. Ted Ward, "The Impossible Dream" message given at Association of Evangelical Relief and Development Organizations annual meeting in Kansas City, Nov. 19-21, 1980.
8. Wade Coggins, and E. L. Frizen Jr., op. cit. p. 167.

7

HOW DID WE GET THERE FROM THERE?

"Doc" Jepson was an innovator—a mover of men—a man ahead of his time. Most people have never heard of this quiet-spoken chiropractor, who lived in Seattle, Washington, far from the traditional places where "things happened" in our evangelical history. But N. A. Jepson was a man who had his sights raised, and with God-given perception sensed a new day coming in missions.

In the early 1940s, foundations were being laid for the explosion of evangelical Christianity in the United States, which would prepare the way for the "fabulous twenty-five years of missions," as Ralph Winter describes them. As if in preparation for the post-war mission boom, when literally dozens of new mission organizations would emerge, businessmen in America began mobilizing their considerable resources for God.

It was in those days that the Gideons and Christian Business Men's Committees (CBMC) were formed; for instance, Jepson was one of the five founding members of the CBMC. Already the "movers" of the coming para-church developments were on the scene—"Sergeant" Theodore Engstrom, a young evangelist Billy Graham, Torrey Johnson—and many of the bow-tied and red-socked young men who precipitated the Youth For Christ movement.

The Jepsons' home was always open to Christian workers and missionaries who were invited to stay in their specially built "prophet's chamber" when passing through Seattle. Jepson's path crossed frequently with those leaders, and he prayed for them and became involved in the grass roots of those movements. But in the recesses of his heart were the stirrings of another groundswell—an idea before its time— that would eventually add a whole new impetus to world missions.

At heart Jepson had a world view of the family of God. Helping to build the church across the sea became his driving passion. He spent hours listening to missionaries' reports, asking perceptive questions of those who enjoyed the refreshment of the Jepson home.

He had a special burden for China—then with a population of some four hundred million people. Born during the time of the Boxer Rebellion, Jepson had grown up on the stories of missionary martyrdom and hatred for Western "foreign devils." But as he listened to reports of courageous and dedicated missionaries who had braved the unpopularity and hardships and rigors of a different language and a different culture, he became convinced that the future of the church in China depended upon "native" evangelists. He was convinced the task of evangelism would never be completed with foreign missionaries alone.

But how could he help these evangelists? How could he make contact with Chinese Christians to lead such a work in China? Everyone to whom he spoke discouraged him. "If the missionaries on the spot did not feel it advisable to fund native evangelists," they assured him, "it should never be done from across the sea." With the growing emphasis on the indigenous church, many mission leaders told him frankly he was behind the times. "The national church must stand on its own feet," was the slogan. It should not be spoiled by financial hand-outs.

Jepson sensed something was missing in the attitude of

many mission leaders: the concept of the equality of the body—that all members were equally endowed with the power and the gifts of the Holy Spirit. He was convinced God could build His Church directly through them if He so chose, and if they needed financial backing, they ought to have some way to receive it.

At one point he was approached by the leader of the "Native Preacher's Company," who funded national pastors directly through missionaries from the United States. But Jepson was uncomfortable with that method, recognizing such direct financial control could hinder the independence of the church, so he continued to wait and pray for the right idea.

In 1943 the pieces came together.

Duncan McRoberts, a CIM missionary to China, had fled ahead of the encroaching Japanese, and came to the United States to rally prayer and interest for the war-ravaged land. His incredible stories of his escape as he traveled with the retreating Chinese army held his audiences spellbound.

Providentially, Duncan McRoberts spoke in the Seattle area, and Cephas Ramquist, a friend of Jepson's, heard him. He called Jepson after the meeting. "You must meet this man; I think he has the information you've been looking for. He knows Chinese evangelists who need help—and he talks like you do."

Jepson was interested and called a few businessmen together to meet with Duncan McRoberts in his home. Listening to the stories of bloodshed and devastation of war, Jepson's heart again responded with anguish to the hopelessness of that vast land without Christ. Convinced that something must be done, Jepson interrupted McRobert's report with the question, "But what's the answer for China? How can we get to the people? Even when the war ends, the aversion to foreigners will continue to be a barrier between us and the Chinese."

McRoberts had a ready reply. "I think my father-in-law, Fred Savage, has the answer. He went from Britain as a missionary to China in 1910. He worked for thirteen years in the traditional manner. Gradually he realized there were Chinese Christians who were capable and dedicated and eager to reach their countrymen for Christ. But they were hamstrung by poverty and lack of opportunity. They couldn't move out of their local community even though they wanted to evangelize other areas. They had no funds to print literature or to buy a train ticket to the next town. My father-in-law was a trained electrical engineer, so he took a job in Shanghai, and gave the funds he received from England to national evangelists. He believes as I do that the 'native' evangelists are the key to winning China."

Early in 1943 the China Native Evangelistic Crusade (CNEC) was incorporated, with Dr. N. A. Jepson as president. It was dedicated to the "winning, training and sending of national leaders to serve the Lord among their own people" (a vision later expanded to include peoples of other tribes and nations). The board of nine businessmen promised to bear all the expenses of administration, promotion, and travel on the American side and send all funds received directly to the field—China.

Meanwhile the final piece of the puzzle was falling into place in the western province of Kweikchow in China. A young evangelist, Calvin Chao, had also fled before the Japanese, moving further into the interior with thousands of other Chinese refugees. While pastoring a small church, his heart became deeply burdened over the unevangelized in the towns and villages of China's vast interior who had never heard of Christ. Sometimes he and his wife and a few Christian friends would go out into a field and pray under a pine tree, weeping for the lost and pleading for a missionary vision for the Chinese church.

For some time Calvin had recognized that insurmountable barriers stood between the lost and the church. Antagonisms toward Western thought and Western missionaries were running high; superstition and tradition held the people in a tight grip; indifference and unwillingness to leave the comforts of the cities (where most of the churches had been established) to endure the hardships of travel to the interior kept the church immobilized.

In later years Calvin Chao wrote in his testimony: "I had the vision, but how little I could do. I was bound to a little church in Kweiyang and could not even leave the city for an evangelistic trip. But I would pray."

God was working to put the pieces together, and Duncan McRoberts, recalling Calvin Chao's evangelistic fervor and organizational ability from his days in China, suggested that the newly formed CNEC board cable Chao, and ask him to organize a board that would oversee the work that would be assisted by CNEC.

Chao records his reaction to that request: "How it astonished me. Its visions were exactly like mine. . . . I could hardly believe my eyes. . . . While I prayed for guidance, God's Word to Gideon came to me with power. Gideon said, 'Oh my Lord, wherewith shall I save Israel? behold, my family is poor in Mannaseh, and I am the least in my father's house. And the LORD said unto him, Surely, I will be with thee, and thou shalt smite the Midianites as one man' (Judges 6:15, 16 KJV)."

With this promise, Chao responded to the call and began forming "evangelistic bands" to go into the interior provinces. The idea of "preaching bands" was not new in China—mission societies had organized such bands to travel into remote areas, staying for a certain period of time until a group of Christians had been discipled. But Chao recognized the need for specialized training for such itinerant evangelists—and his vision included training evangelists as well as sending them out.

The early reports of these bands read like missionary classics. Chao wrote from Anshun in Kweichow Province in April, 1944,

On the fourth day we reached a climax. While preaching the message of salvation, more than half the audience rose to their feet and headed for the altar, weeping bitterly as God's Spirit smote each heart with a realization of the awful debt of sin, and as men and women completely broken in the presence of their crucified Lord, took their place as guilty, hell deserving sinners, names were recorded in the "Lamb's Book of Life."

In January, 1945, Chao reported on the Kaiyang band of thirteen adults and two children who had walked in pouring rain for three days, arriving with blisters on their feet. After calling on the magistrate, the head policeman, and the principals of the schools, they began holding meetings.

In that same month an anonymous report in the *Crusade* (CNEC's news sheet at that time), from a band visiting Hua Chi, a little town with a number of tribal villages surrounding it, read,

While we were preaching, a woman came in bowing and smiling. She took off her bamboo hat and bowed several times saying that she had heard the gospel before and asked the band to go to her home nearby. She told them her story. Something like fifteen years ago a certain colporteur went to her village and preached before he sold the Gospels. She was quite attracted by the preaching and wanted to know more about it, but she has never had a chance since then. When our band went, she recalled that colporteur and she felt so happy that after fifteen years she had for the first time an opportunity to hear about Jesus again . . . after talking with Mrs. Yu, she made her first prayer and was converted.

Within two years' time thirteen gospel bands made up of Chinese evangelists, Bible women, and students were formed. Thirteen gospel halls had been opened. The work extended to five provinces, including Sinkiang, just north of Tibet, which had been closed to the gospel for some time and where missionaries weren't allowed to enter. God opened that door by sending a Christian government worker and his wife. While her husband fulfilled his official duties, Mrs. Lee witnessed and taught the Bible, and soon a church was established.

In 1945 CNEC-assisted workers opened the Spiritual Training Seminary in Chunkung with thirty students. By 1946 a second Bible seminary was opened in Nanking, and by then sixty-five Chinese missionaries were evangelizing and teaching in five provinces. Wherever churches were established, local Christians began supporting their own workers so that the evangelists could go on to reach others. All this was possible because a small new channel was opened to enable them to receive some of the supply that the rest of the family of God (the Church) enjoyed in the West.

With the Japanese surrender late in 1945 there was great optimism in China. After eight years of war and hardship, the Chinese Christians looked forward to a period of rapid growth.

The "refugee universities," which had developed during the war years, were a fruitful harvest field. Calvin Chao was instrumental in starting a nationwide student movement, which later became known as China Inter-Varsity Fellowship. By that time there were more than two thousand students, many of whom had a vision and burden for missionary work among the unevangelized millions of China. Western missionaries began returning to their stations; others who had been interned by the Japanese were released, including Fred Savage and his wife. Fred was then approached by the CNEC board to serve as field superintendent in Shanghai.

The board of directors in Seattle was jubilant that the "idea before its time" had been proven valid. God was enabling the national leaders in China to strategize, plan, implement, and be responsible for a growing work of God in places where the Gospel had never been preached. CNEC publications openly called for people to "sponsor a national evangelist—$20 a month will take care of all his expenses."

But no sooner had the Japanese surrendered than a new wave of war threatened as the Red Army inexorably began pushing Chiang Kai-shek's army south, enveloping town after town in communism. As we noted in chapter one, Paul Chang fled Guilin in 1949 when the takeover was just about complete. By 1951 CNEC evangelistic bands were cut off from further financial assistance. Of the 129 national evangelists, many suffered under the so-called Cultural Revolution; six were martyred, and an unknown number imprisoned.

While Dr. Jepson, Cecil Kettle (who took over the helm of CNEC after Jepson's death in 1951), and the rest of the board struggled with the problems of closed doors in China, exciting new opportunities opened up among one and a half million Chinese refugees who fled to Hong Kong. Later efforts were made among Chinese in Singapore and other parts of Southeast Asia. CNEC extended its ministries beyond the Chinese to other peoples, and by 1961 the name was changed to *Christian Nationals Evangelism Commission* (later shortened to *Christian Nationals*). But during that time the board had to face the reality of a constituency at home that was not yet ready to support independent national ministries. The "idea before its time" may have proven timely as far as the national church was concerned, but mission strategists and pastors, and mission-minded Christians in North American churches still had reservations.

The political changes taking place in China, however, were beginning to have an historical effect on missions, and it was a turning point in the leadership of the national church. Hospitals, schools, and other institutions, valued at hundreds of millions of dollars, were left behind as the missionaries had to leave. The only ones left to carry on the witness were the national Chinese Christians.

In this climate many mission organizations were restructured as mission strategists were recognizing that there was a need to develop a true sense of partnership and interdependence between missions and national churches; hundreds of new agencies were formed. A tidal wave of change politically brought the collapse of "Western messiahship" and developments challenging Western systems of government and economics.

Some denominations and missions worked earnestly to turn the national churches loose so that they might develop their own structures and patterns of witness that would be the most effective for reaching their own people. The impact of these first moves from "paternalism to partnership" was very evident.

During this period the church in Korea captured the world's attention. It was seen as a model of true partnership. The Korean church had, almost from its inception, been in the hands of Korean leadership. Missionaries there were "fraternal workers," working with the Korean church and under its oversight. Resources were made available to the Korean church, and though a devastating war had occurred, the church survived and emerged even stronger. In spite of their own suffering, the Korean believers demonstrated a deep concern for missions. Dr. Edwin Kilbourne, of the Oriental Mission Society, described the mission enthusiasm of Korean believers:

> I have seen our Korean Christians weep because they had nothing more to give. They came forward, emptied their pocketbooks and placed their pocketbooks in the offering, taking their glasses from their eyes, rings from their fingers, clothing from their backs, shoes from their feet, they placed them on the altar and then cried because they had nothing more to give. I have known some to leave the meeting, go to their homes, get their bedding and the remainder of their clothing and bring them saying, "Sell them for the offering." I have seen our precious native preachers, who had come to the conference from 200 miles distance, place their return bus tickets in the offering and say, "Redeem them, and give the money to missions. We will walk home." The Korean church knows how to give.[1]

Today the Korean church is the fastest growing in the world, with six new congregations being officially organized every day and thousands preparing for cross-cultural mission work.

On the other hand, as colonialism was declining in Africa, liberal Christians predicted that the church would recede and perhaps even disappear because it was so closely identified with Western colonialism. Certainly the situation was unstable, but again, in His sovereign grace, God overruled, and about the same time a strong indigenous church began to emerge.

The rapid political changes accelerated the plans most missions already had for the development of national leadership. During the 1960s, the "winds of change" blew across the continent. Forty-five countries gained political independence, and nationalism gave African leaders a new assertiveness. Missions either willingly or unwillingly gave more responsibility to national leadership. On the spiritual level there was less of the "either one or the other" attitude, and more acceptance of each other as equals. A wave of qualified Christian leaders, with sound academic training and intense dedication to Christ, arose. This gave credence to the work of foreign missions, for in spite of problems and weaknesses, they have been basically successful as being God's instrument for planting His Church.

By the early 1970s, some missions shifted policies and began to put more resources into the hands of the national churches, turning ownership of property and control of institutions over to them.

But in spite of these developments, church mission tensions remained one of the most serious problems facing missions in Africa, and endless hours were spent in missionary conferences debating the problems. While the African church resented the dominance and foreignness of the mission-controlled institutions, some missionaries were afraid to give too much control to the African church for fear it could not handle it. For some missions even the first step—to invite national church leaders to attend their annual conference and openly express their own views—became a stumbling block.

Yet, in spite of these tensions, missionaries and church leaders alike were shocked when John Gatu, general secretary of the Presbyterian Church of East Africa, announced a call for moratorium in February, 1971. He wrote, "The answer to our present problems can only be solved if all missionaries can be withdrawn in order to allow a period of not less than five years for each side to rethink and formulate what is going to be their future relationship."[2]

Evangelical leaders, both missionary and African, while admitting the problems existed, rejected the concept of moratorium. Byang Kato succinctly summarized the opposition: "A call for moratorium is merely an emotional appeal without adequate consideration of the ramifications involved. The Church of Christ is one. The unregenerate world is also one. Moratorium is unbiblical and unnecessary."[3]

Yet in the midst of those difficulties there has been phenomenal church growth in Africa during the past few decades. Today 1 out of every 2.5 people in Africa is a Christian. In 1979, alone, there was a net gain of 6 million adult believers in the African churches; that is 16,000 new converts per day!

On the world mission scene, evangelical agencies in the West began to subsidize strategic conferences to enable church leaders in developing nations to benefit from such experiences and dialogue.

However, while nationals were invited initially simply as observers at evangelical conferences, ecumenical conferences had long since included them as full participants. For example, an Indian bishop, V. S. Azariah, gave one of the plenary addresses at the World Missions Conference in Edinburgh in 1910.

The Congress on Worldwide Missions, which convened in Wheaton, Illinois, in 1966, was attended by 938 delegates who represented some 150 mission boards. The congress theme was "The Church's Worldwide Mission." Few sessions, however, actually dealt with the issues and principles of the nature of the church as it relates to the oneness in the body of Christ. Included in the closing pronouncements was the declaration that the implementation of world evangelization is being retarded by too much missionary control.

In 1970 a follow-up consultation at Elburn, Illinois, sponsored by the Evangelical Committee on Latin America

(ECLA), called attention to the damage done by an "overly rigid application of indigenous principles" (legalistic reduction of funds and personnel without due consideration to specific situations and needs). Then, in a commendable effort to continue evaluation, a joint retreat and study conference was co-sponsored in September, 1971, by the Evangelical Foreign Missions Association (EFMA) and the International Foreign Missions Association (IFMA) at Green Lake, Wisconsin. Among the 406 invited delegates and observers were fifteen nationals from overseas.

It was an interesting commentary on the times (and the level of awareness and acceptance of the principle of aid to our brothers in need) to note that at Green Lake the fifteen nationals who were present were given only one session in which they could, as a panel, express themselves, and then only a handful were selected to participate. No national leader was asked to speak in a plenary session or make a major address of any kind. The session they were given was the final hour of the gathering—at a time when a great number of delegates had already left. Others were sitting near the back with their suitcases by the door, ready to rush out to catch rides to the airport.

A number of the national leaders expressed privately that this was an insult to their younger churches—and even to them personally. They felt that the session assigned to them (forty-five minutes for fifteen people) was "tokenism" and an evidence that the leaders in the affluent churches were not yet ready to deal with the principle of mutuality. Commenting on this in an article, "Reflections on GL '71," for the *Evangelical Mission Quarterly*, Hector Espinoza of Mexico wrote,

By the end of the conference it was easy to discover at least one of the causes of tension. Out of 15 national "consultants" only 6 received the opportunity of addressing the conference in a general session, and then strictly only three minutes each. By then, it was obvious to some mission executives and nationals alike, that unfortunately there still widely prevails the old mentality of having the missionary do all the talking and let the national do all the hearing.

Ted Engstrom observed,

Delegates were urged often by the conference leadership to "listen" to the voices from overseas, but, unfortunately, the few men representing national church leadership were a minority and the "listening" process was pretty much one of mission leader "listening" to fellow-mission leader. What "voices" were heard from the overseas national was a plea to hear the cry for "change" from abroad and to have an openness to the "new thing" which the Holy Spirit is doing in His Church in the world today.

The theme at the Congress on Evangelism in Berlin in 1966 was "One Race, One Gospel, One Task." Though this congress dealt primarily with the theology of evangelism and was dominated by Western church leaders in the programming and the speaking, a number of nationals from the developing nations were given some prominence. This gathering, which followed the Wheaton congress by a few months, took a giant step forward in considering the oneness of the church body.

The follow-up congress in Lausanne, Switzerland, in July 1974, where the theme was, "Let the Earth Hear His Voice," evidenced a notable, refreshing, and encouraging shift to acceptance and participation by those whom God had called and ordained from throughout the world. The reports and papers of the congress were published in book form and offered the best, to that date, of wide cross-cultural interaction from around the world. The body of Christ at that congress learned from all its members.

The next major Consultation on World Evangelization was held in 1980, in Pattaya, Thailand. The transition seems to have been almost completed. There was some evidence of Western domination in the areas of organization, expertise in programming and communications (which are legitimate contributions from those of developed nations), but by and large this consultation dealt with the issues confronting the church in the world. The program director was Dr. Saphir Athyal of India. The keynote message was given by Gottfried Osei-Mensah of Ghana. In the plenary sessions there was no evidence of the ascendency of the West, and the participants seemed to feel that they all had an equal voice and opportunity to give full expression to their views and convictions.

In the statement issued at the close of the consultation in Thailand in June, 1980, the participants declared,

. . . we must have a change in our personal attitudes. We have to repent of prejudice, disrespect, and even hostility toward the very people we want to reach for Christ. We have also resolved to love others as God, in Christ, has loved us, and to identify with them in their situation as He identifies Himself with us in ours.

In November of 1980 in Edinburgh a worldwide conference of strictly mission agency delegates was held. While in 1910 no Third World mission agency was officially represented, in the sister conference in 1980 fully one-third of the 171 agencies sending delegates and one-third of the 264 individuals attending were nationals from the Third World. National mission leaders were invited to give three of the four morning plenary addresses. One speaker, Dr. Ralph Winter, predicted that Third World leaders would dominate the world of missions before the end of this century.

And so, in recent years most mission movements have

seen rapid progress in their hopes for indigenous churches that they have been used of God to bring into being. There is a steady shift by most leading evangelical missions away from a legalistic and autocratic approach toward nationals and indigenous work. With this there is a growing sense of partnership and interdependence between missions and national churches. There is more of an attitude of acceptance of each other as equals.

Jepson, who died in 1951, would not have been surprised at the growing groundswell of interest in assisting national leaders to reach their own people for Christ. Even before the evangelical congresses recognized the contributions and importance of national leadership in their own programs, other mission organizations had begun to move in this direction.

Some found this was the only way they could operate. For example, the Slavic Gospel Mission, which was established in 1934, found that doors to North American missionaries were closed in countries like Finland, Poland, and Yugoslavia after the second World War. But national leaders in those countries desperately needed outside assistance as they ministered behind the Iron Curtain.

World-Wide Missions International in Pasadena, California, was founded in 1950 by Basil Miller. It is primarily concerned with supporting national workers, though it has about twenty Western missionaries overseas. There are some five hundred associated churches in thirty-four Third World countries.

AMG International was founded in 1942 by Spiros Zodhiates as the American Mission to the Greeks. It planted churches, distributed literature, and was involved in broadcasting and other support ministries in Greece. Most of the personnel assisted by the mission were nationals. This policy persisted as AMG spread into other countries. Today it has a national staff of about two hundred working in nineteen countries and assists more than twenty-five hundred nationals (including lepers and children as well as church leaders), the majority of whom are in India.

These are just three of a growing number of non-denominational mission agencies whose primary purpose is to support national Christian leaders working in their own countries, indicating a growing interest in providing financial help for the Third World church. A large proportion of these bodies are ethnically oriented and support nationals exclusively in one or two countries.

For example, Evangelize China Fellowship (ECF) assists five hundred Chinese missionaries in Southeast Asia. The mission was started in Shanghai in 1947 by Dr. Andrew Gih. Fleeing before the communists, Gih eventually settled in the United States, where he heads this growing organization whose main emphasis is "to reach Chinese for Christ." Several Western missions loan their missionaries to ECF to help with training the nationals.

Another is Bibles for the World, whose primary emphasis today is to distribute Bibles in the Third World. It also has had a long-standing interest in supporting nationals and establishing national churches. Formerly known as the India-Burma Pioneer Mission, it was instrumental in starting the "Independent Church of Burma," which has grown steadily without foreign missionary assistance. Today Bibles for the World supports more than three hundred national leaders, mostly in India.

Many of these agencies have a limited outreach with annual budgets of less than $100,000. Several are directed by national leaders who have effected incorporation of their agency in the United States so they can raise funds for their ministries overseas. One such agency supports only four nationals.

Most of these organizations cooperate with and appreciate traditional Western missionaries. But a few are antagonistic, declaring that the day of the missionary is past, and that all mission money should go toward supporting nationals.

Besides these agencies, which primarily transmit funds to independent national ministries, are scores of traditional mission agencies that have national workers on their staffs. The Africa Evangelical Fellowship (AEF), for example, has more than 235 North American missionaries and reports that more than five hundred nationals are working in cooperation with it. Though most are supported by local national churches, the mission hires some national personnel in its institutions—this money coming directly from overseas.

A service agency like the World Literature Crusade (WLC), which provides and distributes Christian literature, has a national staff of more than 1,600 who are paid directly through WLC and are responsible to the mission administration. The Navigators have some 250 national coworkers who serve beside their 145 overseas personnel.

Of the many agencies whose primary function is to support national leaders, *Christian Nationals Evangelism Commission,* with its more than forty years of experience, has the broadest commitments. Now working in almost forty countries, it assists some fifteen hundred national leaders as well as aiding education programs from primary through seminary level involving more than twelve thousand students.

Its network of prayer and financial support spreads around the world. In the very early days of the mission, friends of the Savages in England formed a committee, which gradually developed into a strong council, gaining backers for nationals throughout Great Britain.

Likewise, Christians in Australia were assisting Doris

Lum, a young Chinese-Australian working as Calvin Chao's assistant in China. Doris married John Lu and the two served faithfully for many years both in China and in representing the needs in Australia. A committee formed by friends who were assisting John and Doris has since grown into an active Australian council.

In the early 1960s in Canada, Ed Payne, former SIM missionary to Nigeria, was instrumental in establishing the Canadian board, which actively represents the cause of nationals across the northern part of the continent.

Notes

1. Clay Cooper, *Nothing to Win but the World*, Zondervan Publishing House, Grand Rapids, Michigan, 1965, p. 46.
2. Harold Fuller, *Mission Church Dynamics*, William Carey Library, Pasadena, California, 1980, p. 100.
3. Ibid., p. 104.

8

HOW TO DEVELOP A
RELATIONSHIP WITH
NATIONALS THAT WORKS

*Partnership includes the free sharing of all resources
for the proclamation of the Gospel* (Dr. George Peters).

As we have seen in the previous chapter, a growing number of missions are supporting national ministries today. Though each organization doing so has to establish its own guidelines for assistance, it would be helpful to know the procedures followed by a mission that has grappled with the issue for many years.

With its more than forty years of experience in almost forty countries, *Christian Nationals* has developed time-tested procedures for analyzing national ministries, which could serve as a helpful basis of evaluation for others.

One of the hardest things to do is to have to say "no." In one year more than 150 requests came to the office of *Christian Nationals* (over seventy of them from India alone). Each one had to be considered on its own merit, and each one represented a person longing to serve Christ among his own people.

For example, the following is a letter received from Brazil:

Dear Mr. Finley:
  I would like to introduce you to a unique evangelism ministry for which God has given a vision to hundreds of enthusiastic young people here in Rio de Janeiro. . . .

We have a growing vision of what God can do through us. We have begun a lay Bible institute through which 24 young people are now being trained for this missionary work. . . .

We want to form many teams that will be able to stay for up to three months in any place until a group of believers can be formed and placed under the care of the nearest established evangelical church.

Can we ask for your partnership with us?

Or this one is from India:

Dear Mr. Lutz:

The Lord showed me the need for a ministry with a vocational training program which would have an ultimate goal of disciple building. . . . When one completed the training of about two years, he would not only be a matured Christian . . . but also have learned a trade by which he would be able to earn his own living . . . because he was very poor and uneducated he would not have been able to find employment and would have been lost for His service. . . . I have been dreaming, praying and waiting upon the Lord. . . . In 1979 (I) resigned from the bank and stepped out in faith. I am trying to locate a house to rent to have a small carpentry workshop and hand-loom weaving center. I would like to have it partially residential . . . to begin a discipling program.

I shared these burdens with Rev. _____, and he asked me to write to you and tell you about me and see what God could do through your ministry.

How Do They Qualify?

The responsibility for accepting or rejecting ministries for assistance is not taken lightly. It may take anywhere from six months to a year before final approval is given. In one year only ten of the 150 ministries that applied were accepted.

Allen Lutz, vice president for new ministries, who coordinates the research on all these requests, wrote to one candidate:

I am sorry to have to report that *Christian Nationals* is simply unable to expand its involvements any broader in Zaire at this time. We are struggling to strengthen our commitment with the ones that we are already assisting.

You can be assured that this decision is not based on the lack of interest or concern. I find myself waking up early in the morning praying for Zaire. Surely there is a great spiritual conflict going on in your country. Praise the Lord we are on the victory side even though the battle is tough.

Of course many who write us simply don't qualify. Some of the "automatic" rejections go to:

—individuals applying for personal support who are not working under a bona fide national board of directors or church organization.

—a ministry that is simply a "vision" without evidence that some effort has been made to launch the program with the resources at hand.

—individuals seeking assistance to study in the West (though at times help is given to nationals already affiliated with *Christian Nationals,* if their board feels it is necessary for the ministry).

But all inquiries are answered, realizing that each one represents the hopes, dreams, and burdens of God's servants—people who, for the most part, are limited in their service by a lack of resources.

Each agency offering assistance to nationals should consider its own priorities when evaluating national ministries. *Christian Nationals,* for example, is not primarily a relief or development agency, though we have spearheaded some major relief projects; e.g., Guatemala earthquake relief in 1976. But other agencies are better qualified and prepared to handle relief than we are.

Our primary objectives are centered in evangelism, church planting and leadership development, and ministries with these goals are given priority in our consideration.

On the other hand, each culture has distinctive needs that should be considered in determining priorities. For example, France, with its plethora of cathedrals and long history of Roman Catholicism, is generally resistant to public evangelism. But as France is a media-oriented society, Christian T.V. and films have a ready-made audience. Thus when Euro Media Productions requested assistance to purchase expensive T.V. equipment and regular support for staff until it became established, we accepted the proposal. Films and T.V. can serve as a subtle evangelistic tool, preparing the way for others to harvest with more direct methods.

Or consider India, where personal evangelism and door-to-door literature distribution are desperately needed in rural areas, where more than ninety-five percent of the people are not Christian. Such a method would probably not need outside assistance in urban South Africa, where there is a strong evangelical church.

Things to Consider

A careful study of priorities and plans of the ministry being considered can determine how its goals fit into the overall strategies being developed by other Christian leaders and missions for this area.

It goes almost without saying that there must be agreement on basic doctrinal position. Though for many years we simply required a signing of our doctrinal statement, we now find it more helpful to ask the person applying for assistance to write up his own.

The national's relationship with the national church is carefully investigated, for we believe assistance should strengthen the whole body in a community, not intensify divisions.

This can be more difficult than it sounds. For example, we accepted a ministry whose leader was the chairman of a local body of churches, which seemed to indicate that he was well accepted by the church. However, when some members of the local church heard of his new relationship with us, they sent one of their representatives to our office in the United States to explain problems of communications and personality differences. They made it very clear that any new ministry headed by this man would have a hard time gaining acceptance in the Christian community. Sensing that this assistance could prove divisive, we held off making a commitment until the matter was sorted out.

On the other hand, we have assisted a leading evangelist in an African country who had pastored a large church in his denomination. In order to be accepted as an evangelist across denominational lines he had to free himself from being closely associated with one denomination. The church gladly freed him. *Christian Nationals* assisted him to launch a nationwide evangelism ministry, and he continues to receive excellent cooperation and many invitations to minister in his own denomination in which he remains an active member.

Besides the local church, other national bodies, such as the association of evangelicals in the country, mission organizations, and other para-church organizations are contacted for their recommendations. One can't always expect one hundred percent approval, but if the overwhelming tenor of the replies is favorable, it is assumed that the ministry will have no difficulty cooperating with or having its program accepted by the rest of the church.

It is important to evaluate the financial situation of the applying ministry. Has every effort been made to gain local support? Are the requests simply worthwhile or are they really needful? Will they make a measurable difference in the effectiveness of the ministry?

When the Evangelical Fellowship of Kenya asked for assistance, it soon became clear that every effort had been made to raise support from within the country. But it was a "Catch 22" situation. In order to gain the cooperation and support of the churches of all evangelical denominations, a concerted educational program had to be initiated, and benefits demonstrated through the ministry of EFK. But there were no funds to hire a general secretary to initiate the program and plan the education.

Once *Christian Nationals* agreed to back the ministry, Isaac Simbiri, who had been asked to serve as its first full-time secretary, was able to free himself from other responsibilities and set up an office. His well-thought-out plan for educating the churches of Kenya and training in lay leadership is already bearing fruit.

It is also important to know whether the ministry could develop and expand without perpetual outside assistance. A ministry that is too foreign to the culture may not become rooted there, and once outside assistance is withdrawn, the church may be unable to carry it on. This has been the case with some Western mission projects in the past, and national leaders may be prone to do the same.

In our initial "Ministry Proposal" form we also ask for specific goals and objectives (though realizing this is a Western concept which is not an integral part of many national cultures). However, in evaluating the future effectiveness of the ministry, as well as when presenting the financial needs to donors, clear-cut objectives are invaluable. It has been our experience that this requirement has often helped nationals articulate their goals and has been invaluable to them as well.

When Dr. Chris Marantika presented his proposal to establish a seminary in Indonesia, he had written out clearly defined goals and a specific timetable. While completing his seminary work, he had drawn together a staff of four Indonesians and three Western missionaries, two serving with Overseas Crusades, and one with TEAM. The timetable allowed for one year of basic preparations after his return to Indonesia, with the opening of the school to take place in August, 1979. Church planting was to be the touchstone of the new seminary, and each student would be required to plant a church before being graduated.

Goals included: One thousand graduates by the year 2000;

Eleven full-time church planters on the field;

Ten new congregations planted each year;

Three renewal conferences a year;

Four thousand contributors enlisted in Indonesia by 1980.

When after careful and prayerful study it was determined that these were indeed realistic goals and not visionary pipedreams, *Christian Nationals* agreed to back the seminary. As originally planned, the Evangelical Theological Seminary of Indonesia (ETSI) opened in 1979. Not only are the goals being met, but the timetable has been advanced. Within the first four years, 195 home worship services were established in Muslim villages, more than 50 of which have already been turned over as recognized individual church bodies to local denominations. The ETSI staff now hopes to plant one thousand churches in Indonesia by the turn of the century!

Besides evaluating a ministry's goals, we carefully analyze the structure and quality of the national board. In fact, more than one otherwise satisfactory application has been rejected because the board is weak or unable to demonstrate the ability to direct personnel or take responsibility for finances. It is seldom wise to back a "loner"; sometimes such people are launching out on their own because they are under discipline of the church. There should be clear lines of accountability. The board should establish policies, appoint personnel and handle finances, as well as serving as guide and mentor to the national leader.

How to Help Without Hurting

Christian compassion and sharing with other parts of the body of Christ who are in need are clear Scriptural doctrines. The reality of the oneness of the body of Christ, the beauty of spiritual fellowship and the need to share lives and resources cannot be over-emphasized.

The following are guidelines taken from the operating procedures of *Christian Nationals*.

1. Give assistance humbly and lovingly, not in a paternalistic manner. Rather, consider it a precious privilege to be able to share with those who are our equals, often more gifted and capable than we are.

2. Give support to men and women of God who are fully committed to the ministry of the gospel. Such people are not "hirelings." To avoid the "owner-hireling" relationship, assistance must not be used as leverage to force them to do only what we want them to do.

3. Pursue a policy of non-exploitation of nationals. They should not be objects of our pity, nor are they publicity material to build our organization. The North American "success syndrome" can pressurize nationals needing aid, hindering them from a Spirit-led approach to their own culture because *we* need results!

4. Do not unilaterally initiate assistance programs that unwittingly create a paternalistic relationship with the nationals.

5. Avoid interfering in the administration of the indigenous program. Be sure that the ministry is in the hands of capable and proven leaders who have the right to administer the funds.

6. Assistance need not be restricted to a rigid timetable, but careful note should be made of the proportion of local support in ratio to outside help. Open discussions, mutual respect and love contribute significantly to indigenous initiative and self-support.

7. Matching funds are often an inspiration as well as a teaching instrument for the stewardship of national churches. For example, *Christian Nationals* offered to match what Hong Kong refugee Christians could raise to purchase property for the Hong Kong Bible Seminary on a fifty-fifty basis. Before we could fulfill our commitment we received a letter from them saying they had gained over sixty percent and did not think they would need any more of our funds. We never had to raise our fifty percent!

8. Above all, mutual trust must be developed, which is basic to an ongoing relationship that is satisfying to both parties.

A missionary who spent a great deal of time developing personal relationships with nationals was once asked, "What is the most important thing you can learn from a national?" His reply was, "To trust him."

Trust is basic to a sense of oneness in the body. Don Kammerdiener, missionary to Argentina, wrote:

The total independence among Christians must be seen as a carnal and not a spiritual goal . . . the search for the three selves—self-supporting, self-propagating, self-governing—often results in practice in a sterile, stagnate church whose most notable achievement is born and nurtured in an atmosphere of mistrust and egotism. Thankfully, there is another and brighter picture to be seen in today's world. These are the examples of Christians who eagerly sense and glory in their oneness with fellow believers in other lands. They rejoice in the spiritual fellowship and yet increasingly rely on the spiritual resources made available by God for the carrying out of their task, accepting as part of those resources the lives and money given by Christians in other lands.[1]

Signing a Reciprocal Commitment

Once a project is accepted, respresentatives of *Christian Nationals* and of the national ministry sign a "Reciprocal Commitment," which spells out the "give and take" expected of each, based on mutual self-esteem and respect.

A reciprocal commitment implies that each party to the agreement receives benefits and shares in the responsibility of reaching a mutual goal. John Janson, a Christian anthropologist, warns about giving and receiving:

Whenever generosity of giving, teaching and helping is of unconditional character, the recipient must be able to return the gift of some equivalent in order to retain his own respectable self. Otherwise he will begin seeing himself as inferior to the giver; his personal sense of worth is downgraded and instead of being grateful, he will be bitter.[2]

In *Christian Nationals'* "Reciprocal Commitment" the breakdown of responsibilities is as follows:
The national ministry agrees:
1. To adhere to basic Bible doctrines held to by *Christian Nationals* and other associated indigenous ministries.
2. To strive for self-support and to maintain its indigenous nature.

3. To limit any appeal made for funds outside of its own nation or area through *Christian Nationals* to avoid confusion; this includes all mailings or personal letters appealing for funds.

4. To seek prior agreement from *Christian Nationals* before obligating the organization for any new project or extension of the ministry that will need outside help.

5. To do any overseas deputation in full agreement and under established deputation program of *Christian Nationals*, and to channel funds so raised through the mission.

6. To communicate at least three times a year with sponsors; to provide pictures, reports and other materials so that the mission can gain interest and support.

7. To use funds as designated and to publish an audited financial report annually and send copy to *Christian Nationals*.

8. To permit international president or his appointees to visit work.

9. To fill out questionnaires and evaluation forms as requested by *Christian Nationals*.

Christian Nationals agrees:

1. To pursue a policy of non-exploitation of nationals.

2. To transfer funds provided through God's people with utmost care for work, as designated.

3. Not to interfere with the administration of indigenous programs.

4. To send budgeted and special project funds to the recognized indigenous board (not to an individual) as God provides.

5. To make needs of national ministries known and seek to raise support in a manner honoring to the Lord.

6. To arrange deputation schedules, advance initial expenses, and provide literature and other materials to present the national ministry.

7. To give full explanation of the relationships of the national ministries with other missions in its publicity so as not to confuse the Christian public.
8. To share ideas and literature, provide seminars, etc., to contribute to effectiveness of work if desired.

(A full copy of the Reciprocal Commitment developed by *Christian Nationals* may be found in the appendix.)

Because of this careful concern for the independence and mutual assistance between national and mission, *Christian Nationals* has had a remarkably smooth history between mission and national leaders. For example, Dr. Chris Marantika wrote:

> But what can I say about *Christian Nationals* who assists us so faithfully? Three years have passed since we became associated with them. There is no mission board I know of in the world today that has such full confidence in national workers. . . . Their love, attitude, and words of encouragement increase my faith to claim Indonesia for Christ in this generation.

How Do You Monitor Such Far-Flung Commitments?

With the best of relationships, and the finest of committed leaders, it is still important to monitor national ministries and to know what God is doing in and through them. This enables us to report knowledgeably to those who have entrusted us to deliver their assistance to developing churches.

Along with *Christian Nationals*, almost every other organization that assists nationals includes the following steps to monitor and evaluate the projects that they help:

1. *Field leaders.* Some organizations have more than others, depending upon the independence given to the projects they are helping. *Christian Nationals* has a number of

national area coordinators who are directly responsible to the mission.

In India, for example, our administrative control does not extend beyond the coordinating office. Dr. Arthur Dalavai coordinates our assistance to ministries in four countries in the Asian subcontinent. He has close relationships with leaders of the Indian church, institutions of leadership training, and the evangelical fellowships. He also has had long-standing contacts with many of the evangelical mission groups in these countries. Thus he is able not only to help in the initial research of possible new projects, but in the follow-up of ministries already associated with *Christian Nationals*.

2. *Written reports and audits are required of all ministries on a regular basis.* In addition, a yearly self-evaluation form is sent out, asking for reports on how goals and objectives for the past year were met, and for projected goals and objectives for the future. Each national leader is expected to fill this out for his/her ministry, and a staff member at international headquarters takes time to respond with encouragement and suggestions.

3. *Regional conferences* with leaders of the ministries and *Christian Nationals* administrative staff are held.

4. *Visits to field ministries* by members of the international administrative staff or representatives from other national councils in Australia, Canada, and Great Britain, serve as times of encouragement and mutual blessing. Often new needs and concerns come to light in these visits and serve as fuel for prayer. Information is gathered for publications and sharing with sponsors. On occasion, discrepancies are discovered. Often the national can share problems, burdens, weaknesses, and dreams, when he meets face to face with a mission leader, that he may not feel free to share in writing. Field visits by mission personnel give reality to

reporting and are essential to maintaining credibility with friends and supporters.

Similar guidelines and procedures have been developed by most credible missions involved in support of nationals. Shortcuts can only lead to frustration and disappointments. But following carefully and prayerfully developed procedures can result in a rewarding partnership to build the church around the world.

Notes

1. Don Kammerdiener, quoted in "Our Readers' Opinions," *Evangelical Missions Quarterly*, Vol. 13, No. 2, April 1977, p. 113.
2. Levi O. Keidel, "The Peril of Giving," *World Vision*, November, 1971, p. 8.

9

WHAT ARE THE RESULTS OF ASSISTING NATIONALS?

The new church was dedicated in February, 1981, with great fanfare and rejoicing. For years the congregation had been meeting in homes, rented halls, and even a funeral home—dividing into groups and spreading out across the city wherever they could find a meeting place.

They had been raising funds for their own building since 1969, and over the twelve years their building fund had grown to more than $335,000, enough to put up the modern sanctuary seating five hundred people.

During those same years, their giving to foreign missions also increased—from $868 a year to the present annual budget of $40,000. In 1975 the church treasurer stated in his fiscal report: "We have given away to missions so far, almost the equivalent of our total building fund. But the Lord has blessed our church, and we have not suffered."

In that same year the church stated in its goals: "Our aim should be at least 55 percent of our budget for foreign missions. . . . in addition our young people should go." By 1977, fifteen members were in full-time missionary work or training—including a surgeon and his wife who had gone to Africa under the Sudan Interior Mission.

This *could* be the story of many evangelical churches across America (though very few give over forty-seven percent of their budget to missions). But this *is* the story of the

Bartley Christian Church of Singapore. Bartley began as a house church in 1969 with the encouragement of John Lu, then field director for CNEC in Singapore, and several students from a local high school who had been converted. For a number of years the church received financial help from *Christian Nationals*.

Today the church is not only fully self-supporting, with its own beautiful sanctuary and a broad interest and involvement in missions, but it also continues to support the outreach ministries of CNEC in Southeast Asia.

In fact the *Christian Nationals* associated ministries in Southeast Asia (known there as CNEC) remarkably demonstrate what can happen when a true partnership in missions emerges between East and West. It is interesting to recall that in the early days of this church, some Westerners discouraged *Christian Nationals* involvement, saying, "If you give them money, they'll never help themselves."

The Southeast Asia headquarters is "owned and operated" by a Singapore board. Bartley Church is one of seven fast-growing and enterprising churches that have grown out of this ministry. In fact, a church growth study reveals that CNEC churches are the fastest growing in Singapore, with a 498 percent increase over the past ten years. For example, Toa Payoh Bible Church, begun in 1970, holds five services every Sunday to accommodate its overflowing crowds and gives more than fifty percent of its budget to missions.

The Southeast Asia headquarters has initiated ministries in Indonesia, Malaysia, Burma, and Thailand. Evangelists are sent into primitive, tribal areas; schools have been opened; hundreds of children enabled to attend Christian schools (through the Sponsor-A-Child program); and churches have been planted. Teams of young people from Singapore spend their vacations ministering in these areas; some have gone to work full time. Singapore Christians sponsor hundreds of children so they can attend school. Most of the seven churches associated with the CNEC headquarters there are helping several of their own young people go to Bible school. Many attend the Laymen's Short Term Bible School, which is sponsored by the headquarters. A thriving tape ministry, lending library, and correspondence course operate out of the headquarters— primarily supported through sales and donations from local Christians. Hundreds of these tapes are finding their way into China now.

But the continued involvement of Western Christians enables these enterprising and dedicated national workers to stretch themselves and accelerate their outreach into areas of the community or other countries where Christ is not known.

After all, Southeast Asia is still less than 10 percent Christian (Thailand is .5 percent). But since there are many Chinese in these countries, Singapore Christians can go almost anywhere and be understood, be absorbed into the culture, and relate to the people. Rather than stifling or "spoiling," our dollars (or pounds) have encouraged the creative development of opportunities; and our prayers as interested members of the body of Christ have undergirded this effective ministry.

1. *One of the encouraging results of wisely assisting national ministries is that they can become self-supporting, though they may continue to need help because of the challenge of vast unreached people and areas around them.*

When *Christian Nationals* began work among the refugees in Hong Kong in 1950, the people were destitute and helpless. Almost immediately the dire need for schools for the masses of refugee children was seen as a great opportunity. At one time *Christian Nationals* assisted seven primary schools, sponsoring several thousand children as well as subsidizing buildings and operational expenses.

Today the education department of the CNEC association in Hong Kong is basically self-supporting, and we are phasing out the Sponsor-A-Child program there. As the Hong Kong government provided more education, outside help could be cut back. The government was so pleased with the quality of education in these Christian schools that it was happy to put the administration and staffing of these schools into the hands of Christian organizations such as CNEC. Recently a large grant from the estate of a Christian family in Hong Kong allowed the education department of CNEC to build a second Christian high school there. A previously established school provides quality education for over one thousand students and is a fertile breeding ground for new Christians. Launching the hopeless refugees into an education program resulted in a highly respected, self-supporting network of Christian schools. Several self-supporting churches have grown out of the school program.

2. *Assisting national ministries can result in ministries that become established and respected in the community.*

In 1954 Olympic runner Virgilio Zapata returned to his native Guatemala after completing his studies in North America. As he ministered in evangelism, his heart was touched by the hopeless poverty of his people. His concern for the uneducated children of Guatemala crystallized into what others said was an "impossible dream"—a Christian school that would provide quality education for Guatemalan youngsters.

The skeptics were proven wrong, and today the Instituto Evangelico America Latina (IEAL) is the largest Christian school in all of Latin America, with some five thousand children and young people from kindergarten through high school and a business school.

The board of IEAL struggled for ten years on its own, raising funds in Guatemala and North America. But in

1964 the school was about to close because of financial difficulties when *Christian Nationals* agreed to help. The purchase of IEAL's campus in the heart of Guatemala City reads like a miracle story, with last minute answers to prayer as *Christian Nationals* was able to help raise the fifty-thousand-dollar down payment hours before the deadline.

Today IEAL has a staff of almost two hundred, with six highly qualified principals for the various schools. Many of the staff members, including Superintendent Manfred Hernandez, are IEAL graduates. Less than ten percent of the school's budget now comes through outside sources. In fact, the Guatemala City campus is virtually self-supporting, except for scholarships for needy children and some staff assistance.

IEAL offers a varied program that has produced Christian leaders of all segments of Guatemalan life—from doctors, lawyers, and teachers to the director of Campus Crusade's "Here's Life" campaign.

Graduates of the school are highly respected and have left their mark in every strata of society. But without that initial help and faithful support, especially in its earlier years, IEAL may never have become the stable and influential Christian witness that it is. Today the need for more assistance is basically in the areas of outreach into smaller towns, development programs, literacy classes, and primary schools for poverty-stricken people.

3. *Assisting nationals can result in outreach into unreached areas where the church is too small to sustain any kind of organized ministry.*

One of these unreached areas is Rajasthan—the land of the Rajahs. For centuries these warrior kings ruled over the hot desert sands of northwestern India. They lived in sumptuous sandstone palaces, surrounded by manicured gardens fragrant with lotus flowers and bouganvillas.

The veiled ladies of the harems peered through latticed walls, watching the regal peacocks strut in the gardens below, their raucous calls belying their beauty. They saw their men go off to battle in heavy armor, charging the enemy under the searing sun.

Under British rule, the Rajahs were left undisturbed, for by keeping the balance of power they helped the colonists maintain order in this far-flung corner of India.

To pacify the Hindu Rajahs, very few Christian missionaries were allowed to enter the province. The capital city of Jaipur may look like Bethlehem with its square, flat-roofed houses and its arrogant camels moving regally through the dusty, peopled streets, but the Son of Bethlehem was never introduced here.

In 1950 the British left, and the Rajahs began to lose their wealth and power. A few more missionaries trickled into the province, but were met with disinterest and distrust.

Rajasthan's thirty million people are locked into their "god shelves," their grotesque images of worship, their sacred trees, their caste and their predestined fate. In almost thirty years of sporadic missionary effort only *one-tenth of one percent* admit to being Christian, and thirty-five churches serve the entire population!

But God gave an Indian man, who had trained to become a Brahmin priest before his conversion, the burden to reach this "spiritual desert" for Christ. Gifted with leadership and organizational abilities, Anand Chaudhari designed a strategy that would expose every person in the major towns of Rajasthan to the gospel.

Armed with maps, statistics, and the names of evangelists ready to work with him, Anand presented his vision to *Christian Nationals.* He had already opened a Hindi-speaking Bible school and was receiving overwhelming responses to his weekly radio broadcasts. But Projects 78 and 79 (named after the number of towns the teams would blanket in those two years) were beyond the financial ability of the miniscule church in Rajasthan.

Sharing as partners in this incredible outreach became a most fascinating experience. To think that so few dollars (fifty dollars a month per evangelist) could produce such far-reaching results!

Exciting stories and reports kept coming. For example, Anand wrote of the experiences of the team when it visited the town of Bharatpur:

When our team began distributing literature, a crowd gathered. They were in an ugly mood, surrounding the two young evangelists and pulling at the bags on their shoulders. "We don't want any of your Christian teaching here," they shouted. "We have our own gods in this town. We don't want to hear about any foreign religion."

A scuffle started, and two of the evangelists lay sprawling on the ground, their literature packets spewed out into the dusty street, trampled under the feet of the angry mob. Realizing that they couldn't continue witnessing in the area any longer that day, they gingerly retrieved whatever literature they could and retreated back to their room.

That night the eight young men met to discuss the problem. One evangelist reports, "We prayed about it and got encouragement from the Lord . . . and the next day we started work again . . . once again we got a few slaps . . . they warned us 'unless you leave the town, the consequences will be drastic' . . . but we were encouraged by the Holy Spirit and the Word of God, and again we started working."

While in some areas the teams faced opposition, in others Hindus invited them to hold meetings. An evangelist wrote, "We went to the temple of the Hindus, there also we preached the Gospel and sang there praises of the Lord Jesus Christ."

It almost read like the "Acts of the Apostles"—from beatings and threats to the joyous welcome of the isolated Christians.

From 1978 through 1980 the young evangelists under the leadership of Anand Chaudhari visited 750,000 homes in 157 towns. Sixty thousand people wrote in requesting Bible correspondence courses, many indicating that they had accepted Christ as a result of reading the literature. A surprising number were Muslim and Hindu women, an almost unheard of response in India.

In 1981 Chaudhari implemented the next phase of the program; to send teams of evangelists back into the areas where there had been the most response, to encourage new believers and to establish house churches. By the end of 1982, twenty-one preaching points had been established. Their goal was to plant fifty churches within five years.

4. *Assisting nationals can result in freeing a gifted servant of God to minister to his greatest potential.*

While Gus Marwieh was studying in the United States his driving purpose was to return to his primitive tribal people deep in the bush of eastern Liberia. He had grown up there, having never worn a stitch of clothes until he was fourteen years old. He'd never heard of God, or Jesus Christ, or seen a church or heard a hymn until that fateful day when his mother sent him to live with an uncle in a town near the coast.

There he met not only Christ, but also a black American missionary, Mother Eliza George, who saw Gus's potential and trained and discipled him to take over her work. However when Gus finally returned to Liberia, his plans were detoured. Dr. William Tolbert, then vice president of the country, requested him to teach in the prestigious Ricks Institute in the capital city of Monrovia—and who could refuse such a demand?

After four years, Gus could stand it no longer—the needs of his people, and the struggles of his eighty-six-year-old spiritual mother, who was still carrying on the work alone, were too much. He resigned from Ricks (with the blessing of Dr. Tolbert) and returned to Sinoe County. By this time he was married and had two children, and the decision to step out in faith without any financial backing took a lot of courage.

The Marwiehs received an ecstatic welcome. Gus described it in a letter to his friends in North America: "What a welcome! The jubilation of my first visit was nothing compared to the love poured out to me and my family when my tribe learned that I had come home to stay. From surrounding villages miles away, groups came in day after day bringing gifts of rice, chicken, goats, and cassavas. We received so many chickens that we had to build a special house to keep them. For a month the celebrations continued, and we had enough food to keep our family for the rest of the year. That was God's first answer to our prayer for provision for our family."

Gus was a man of great dreams for his people, and provisions of produce for his family did not answer the need for schools, medical clinics, Bible translation, and church planting that God had placed in his heart. With an average annual income of less than seventy-five dollars, the tribal families could never provide the tools and personnel Gus needed to implement his program.

But with the help of *Christian Nationals*, a far-reaching ministry has grown out of ENI Mission: five primary and two high schools were built and staffed, one hundred churches planted throughout Sinoe and Grand Gedeh County (and several even in the Ivory Coast), a medical clinic was opened on the main station, a technical school to give young people skills as well as Bible training, annual short-term training programs of continuing education for pastors (many of whom are semi-literate) were initiated. And with the assistance of TEAR Fund in the Netherlands, improved cocoa, coffee and rice farms, and poultry projects were developed in some of the poorest areas.

It would be difficult to imagine what Gus Marwieh would have been able to accomplish if he had not received the partnership of resources and prayers of a concerned Christian "family" in the West. Chickens and cassavas don't go very far to build schools or support evangelists.

5. *Assisting nationals can result in stimulating them to become involved in missions in other parts of the world.*

More and more the "whole body" concept of the church is being demonstrated around the world as different members contribute and respond to one another, reacting to each other's needs as surely as the hand flies up to defend the face from attack, or the adrenalin shoots through the system in a crisis.

We have referred frequently in this book to the astounding church growth in Korea today. Operation Lighthouse, an independent church growth movement, which arose as an offshoot of the Presbyterian Church in Korea, demonstrates one way in which this growth is taking place.

Operation Lighthouse was the brainchild of a missionary-national team that has been working together for twenty years in Korea. Serving with the Presbyterian church, Hugh Linton and his co-worker, Ki Chang Ahn, were deeply concerned about the spiritual barrenness of rural Korea.

After doing intensive research, Ahn published a book listing all the areas in rural Korea without a Christian church. He pinpointed some sixteen hundred villages of five hundred people or more who have no gospel witness whatsoever. Added to the problem was the fact that the trained pastors migrate to the cities where there are large churches and better paying positions. Furthermore, loneliness and isolation made the village ministry unattractive and difficult.

Operation Lighthouse utilizes a unique partnership of urban and small town churches of many denominations in Korea with *Christian Nationals* to gain support for their fifty-five church planters. Each supplies one-third of a church planter's salary.

Most of these church planters are trained in small, local Bible schools which meet in a centrally located church building for three or four days of the week. This enables the church planter to return to his village parish each weekend and keeps him from the inevitable disorientation of city life.

After five years these churches must be financially independent and support the church planter as pastor, or he moves on. Operation Lighthouse believes that if they are not on their feet after the church building is up five years, the problem is not financial.

After six years, 120 churches had been established, many with their own church buildings (for which they received an initial thousand-dollar grant). *Christian Nationals* is assisting forty-one church planters and thirty Bible school and seminary students who are preparing to enter the church planting ministry.

But another exciting development is occurring. Larger, more affluent urban churches in Korea are also concerned about the need for evangelism and church growth in other parts of the world. They support more than sixty workers in India, Bolivia, Brazil, Bangladesh, Kenya, etc., by sending their support through *Christian Nationals*.

The churches in Korea are praying for and communicating with their missionaries in other parts of the world, cementing the bond of love that they initiated with their gifts. A letter from one Korean church to an African evangelist reads,

Dear Felix Maafo:

Greetings in the name of Jesus Christ. We were very glad to receive your letter two weeks ago. We had it translated into Korean, put on the wall, and read by all the church members. We were much impressed by your letter. It was very difficult to understand the postage situation in Ghana.

We are very glad to know you in Jesus Christ. We hold divine services in the church at dawn of every day, on every Sunday, and in the evening of every Wednesday. And we pray for you and the stability of your country during every service. Let us do our best, for doomsday is near.

We are helping the missionary works of ten areas in Africa. We can help even more activities if it brings forth a good fruitful result. Let us work to the utmost of our strength even through the difficulties of these latter days.

Looking forward to the bountiful harvest occurring in people's hearts these days. May God bless you.

Yours on a mission in Korea.

Kim Shi-Won

These are just a few case histories from effective national ministries that have demonstrated the value of sharing our resources with them. Not all ministries, of course, can become self-supporting in five years—or even twenty, for that matter. In some areas the dire poverty of the people and the resistance to the gospel necessitates a longer involvement. For many national operations, outside assistance makes the difference between stagnation and new outreach.

In chapter 6 we discussed the possible difficulties encountered in assisting nationals. Obviously the results are not always as encouraging or dramatic as we have described here. Sometimes there is failure and defeat; sometimes overdependence or materialistic motives; sometimes stagnation and apathy permeates a ministry.

Any partnership requires give and take, understanding and forgiveness. Dr. George Peters stated it well when he wrote,

Partnership in missions is a sacred and comprehensive concept of equals bound together in mutual confidence, unified purpose and united effort, accepting equal responsibilities, authority, praise and blame, sharing burdens, joys, sorrow, victory and defeat.[1]

When we share our resources with our brothers and sisters in other parts of the world, the whole body benefits in a visible demonstration of love and unity, no matter what the number of conversions or churches planted might be. And this oneness is a result the world still needs to see.

Notes
1. George W. Peters, *A Biblical Theology of Missions*, Moody Press, Chicago, 1972, p. 238.

10

COOPERATING WITH OTHER MISSIONS IN SUPPORT OF NATIONALS

Caesar Molebatsi returned to his homeland of South Africa during the 1976 riots to take up the leadership of Youth Alive, a youth ministry through which he was converted and nurtured. The modern, attractive youth center in the middle of Soweto just outside of Johannesburg was the hub of activities for hundreds of young people, and the spawning ground for thousands of new Christians over the years.

Caesar had been concerned about the safety of the center, for the pent-up frustrations of the Soweto demonstrators were hurled against any "white-run" organization— primarily government offices and buildings, though others with white connections were also in danger.

But Youth Alive buildings were spared. Though planted and developed by Western missionaries of the Africa Evangelical Fellowship, it had been turned over to a board of African leaders just three years earlier. Caesar had been studying in the United States at the time, but now he had turned to his home to take up his appointed duties as director of Youth Alive. In those three years the youth ministry had gained credibility with the black community; the staff was entirely African, the programs designed and run by Africans. In the minds of the Youth Alivers and the people of Soweto, it was "ours."

There was just one serious drawback. Soweto's black

youth could never support the program without outside assistance.

When the missionaries left the work, they urged their supporters: "Back Caesar and his staff so that the work can continue to reach these strategic young people." But Western Christians hesitate to invest in independent organizations, especially when they are ten thousand miles away, and there is no way to monitor what is going on.

Why didn't the mission that started Youth Alive continue to support it financially, now that it was under the supervision of its own board and with its own black leadership? This is a question many national leaders ask, and one with which many missions have grappled. There are a number of good reasons for withholding such assistance, though national leaders may not always agree as to their validity.

1. *Mission Policy.* For many missions the gradual development of independence for the "daughter churches" and para-church organizations was a long and difficult process. In earlier years most missions heavily subsidized the national churches they planted, appointing pastors, paying their salaries, and putting up their buildings. It is not unusual even today for a national leader to accuse missionaries of "not teaching us how to give." Though, to be perfectly fair, the national church often made little effort to pay its own way, even after years of teaching and encouragement.

Gradually mission leaders took note of this dilemma, putting more emphasis on the need to be self-governing, self-propagating and self-supporting. In the mission classic, *Missions at the Crossroads,* published in 1954, veteran missionary Stanley Soltau stated emphatically, "It cannot be over-emphasized that, regardless of the social and economic standards of the people, it should be understood that they are able to bear this responsibility (self-support) unaided from the beginning."[1]

Thus most missions began writing policies on self-support into their programs—gradual decrease of assistance and eventually legalistically refusing help, as Soltau put it "with no exceptions." This was seen to be for the good of the church, to strengthen it and to develop independence. After all, if missionaries were to work themselves out of a job, they had to leave a financially viable as well as spiritually mature church behind.

Missions did, however, continue to pay salaries for assistants, drivers, house boys, laborers, etc., who worked for the mission, but few acknowledged the rightness and the wisdom of assisting the national in their own programs, which *they* designed, planned, and implemented. This was not accepted policy.

The exceptions to this were several mainline denominations who had from the early years been giving assistance to their national churches with a sense of mutual reciprocity.

2. *Setting a Precedent.* Even when missions saw that certain projects were worthy of support and could not carry on without it, they were fearful of setting a precedent. After all, how could they explain to one daughter church why they could not help her, and yet assist the program of another? How could they support one gifted, dedicated worker in his program of evangelism, etc., and deny help to another? There would be jealousy between the workers and the accusation of having "missionary pets." Church-mission tensions were difficult enough without adding this dimension.

3. *Machinery Lacking.* As the pendulum began to swing from total independence to interdependence and partnership, some missions recognized that certain areas of the national church—for example, outreach into unreached areas and new projects—needed overseas support. But they did not have the machinery to raise this support.

Missionaries in so-called "faith" missions are responsible to raise their own support, and a good bit of deputation time is spent visiting churches and presenting their growing needs. With inflation running rampant everywhere, even long-term missionaries with strong financial bases find they must increase their pledges. It is difficult enough to gain needed support so that they can return to the field, without adding the burden of assistance for national or independent ministries.

The faith mission as an organization, on the other hand, generally does not have discretionary funds available to allocate to independent national projects, and few have representatives who can make the needs of nationals known. Then, too, they do not have machinery to evaluate, monitor, and report on national projects to donors. It would mean developing a whole new emphasis, involving staff and additional finances.

4. *Responsibility to Donors.* Mission organizations, generally, are extremely conscientious about handling the funds given by their supporting friends. Receipting is done with careful observance of IRS regulations. Donors are assured that funds will be used as designated—and, above all, that ministries on the field adhere to the doctrines and ethical standards of the funding body. It is more difficult to make these assurances when funds are given to totally independent, self-governing ministries in another culture. Unless safeguards, such as those described in the reciprocal commitment in chapter eight, are built into the policies, these assurances cannot conscientiously be given.

Thus it is understandable that the Africa Evangelical Fellowship, like so many of its sister missions, did not feel it could continue to be financially responsible for Youth Alive, once it was no longer directed by one of its missionaries. However, even now when gifts specifically designated for Youth Alive are sent into the mission, they are transferred to the field. But without deputation, regular reports, and presentation of needs, there is little hope of maintaining such support.

In God's good timing, however, Caesar met a representative of *Christian Nationals* while he was studying in the United States, and applied for assistance for Youth Alive work. After a field visit and the usual processing procedures, *Christian Nationals* agreed to assist Youth Alive in making its needs known within the larger family in the body of Christ until it could gain enough support from within South Africa.

Today the program reaches about one thousand young people in its weekly clubs in Soweto and almost that many in its branch in KwaZulu. The staff of seven Africans trains young people in leadership of clubs, helps churches develop their own youth programs, runs camps and retreats, and works closely with Bible clubs in all the high schools of Soweto and several in KwaZulu. A ministry to couples, including premarital counseling, and marriage guidance, has been added to aid the deteriorating situation among young families in Soweto. A larger portion of the budget now comes from black young people, and "alumni" of the program—but it is still a long way from being fully self-supporting. Without the help of *Christian Nationals* it could probably have maintained the "status quo" but could never have developed into the far-reaching program it is becoming.

This pattern has been repeated many times as more and more traditional mission boards have approached *Christian Nationals* to assist one of the ministries they have planted, which is now independent but financially in need.

For example, the Africa Inland Church (outgrowth of the AIM) asked not only for assistance for the missionaries to the Giriamas (see chapter three), but also for help in its mission outreach into the Maasai and Turkana tribes, for whom they had been greatly burdened, but because of lack of finances had been unable to send workers. With partial subsidy through *Christian Nationals* they were able to send the volunteers to these unreached tribes.

Assistance was also requested by the Evangelical Church of West Africa (ECWA), established by the Sudan Interior Mission. ECWA, which became autonomous in 1976, is a leader in Third World missions, with over four hundred national missionaries sent out by the church cross-culturally into other tribes of Nigeria.

In 1980 an astonishing new opportunity arose. The Maguzawas, an offshoot of the predominantly Muslim Hausas of northern Nigeria, began to demonstrate a responsiveness to the gospel. The Maguzawas had never assimilated the teaching of Islam—their name means "runners from Islam"—but now they were expressing a desire to have Christians come and teach them about Jesus. ECWA pastors responded, and a program was set up whereby they would leave their churches and move their families north, planning to stay long enough to establish a church. In 1980 all fifty-eight graduates of the ECWA Bible School volunteered to move into the responsive Hausa villages where living conditions were difficult at best. ECWA, however, had reached its limit. Through SIM they approached *Christian Nationals* for help, which enabled more of the new workers to enter this ripe harvest field.

Some years earlier *Christian Nationals* had joined hands with SIM to assist the ECWA church among the Ibo people. After the devastating civil war in the 1960s, the countryside was ravished and the people suffered greatly. Outside assistance was needed to help the impoverished pastors until the Ibo churches could get over the effects of the war.

Once the hard-working Ibos were back on their feet again, there was no need for continued subsidies, and funds were withdrawn to be used elsewhere.

The Sudan Interior Mission illustrates the growing trend on the part of traditional faith missions to assist the independent ministries which have grown out of the work of the mission. In 1976 SIM turned the full responsibility of the work, which the mission had begun almost ninety years before, over to the ECWA church—a process that had begun as far back as 1954.

Harold Fuller, in his book *Mission-Church Dynamics*, describes the rationale behind SIM's present financial policy in relation to ECWA:

> The church is working on trying to be self-reliant. It has been for many years, as far as its pastors are concerned. This has always been the policy of SIM and ECWA—except in exceptional cases. . . . The churches are supporting their pastors and sending out missionaries. They are also contributing to some ministries, such as radio evangelism over ELWA. They are beginning to contribute to the support of their vernacular Bible schools. However, there are still major projects for which support is needed, and which the churches (most of them rural) cannot yet undertake—if they did, it would harm their support of their own missionaries and pastors.[2]

Like SIM, a majority of mainline denominations have long since given autonomy to their churches, and many have continued to assist the younger churches and parachurch agencies financially.

On the other hand, an increasing number of faith missions are offering assistance in varying degrees where they see the younger churches need help and are unable to take advantage of their opportunities without it.

The Latin American Mission, an innovator in this area, gave its churches autonomy almost twenty years ago. In

1971 it set up the Community of Latin American Evangelical Ministries (CLAME in Spanish)—a group of thirteen autonomous organizations engaged in publishing, theological education, and evangelism. LAM describes itself as a "service agency for Latin American ministries," offering assistance without control or dominance.

Paul Pretiz, former general secretary of CLAME, perceptively describes the basis upon which nationals will accept foreign help without resentment or loss of dignity. He explains: "In the churches and institutions, control must clearly be in the hands of the nationals. And once this control is established, they can request foreign resources in their own initiative and terms."[3]

To take such a step involves certain risks. In discussing mission patterns in his book *Mission-Church Dynamics* Harold Fuller points out that "the image of LAM as a strongly evangelical mission was threatened because the seminary, as a separate autonomous member without any church control, invited professors of diverse doctrinal background to join the faculty, thus changing its theological emphasis."[4] In fact, by 1981 LAM had to officially sever its connections with the Latin American Biblical Seminary because of the doctrinal position of some of its staff.

Such risks may be one of the reasons why many traditional missions hesitate to support independent daughter churches and institutions. Yet there is evidence of a growing trend to give assistance, and when they cannot, because of lack of funding or because policy or field situations contradict this, they are turning to missions like *Christian Nationals.*

Whether the mission or the younger church makes the appeal of assistance, *Christian Nationals* attempts to consult closely with all involved, to give credit in all its communications and publications to the parent mission, and to carefully evaluate the benefits and repercussions of this assistance before committing itself to help.

Notes

1. T. Stanley Soltau, *Missions at the Crossroads*, Van Kampen Press, Wheaton, Illinois, 1954, p. 22.
2. Harold W. Fuller, *Mission-Church Dynamics*, William Carey Library, Pasadena, California, 1980, p. 220.
3. Paul Pretiz, "Church-Mission Tensions Today," *Latin America Evangelist*, March-April, 1980.
4. Fuller, op. cit., p. 39.

11

HOW WE CAN SHARE OUR
RESOURCES WITH THE CHURCH
AROUND THE WORLD

Once convinced of the value of supporting and sharing in the ministry of national leaders, the next step is to find a way, either personally or through the local church to become meaningfully involved.

Dr. Paul Smith of Peoples Church in Toronto, Canada, was not convinced for a long time. He admits, "There was a time when I wasn't so sure about national Christians. I thought missionaries from Europe and North America were the only people who could do a first-rate job of spreading the Gospel. I really believed we would spoil nationals if we gave them financial help and responsibility. In fact, I wondered if they could really be trusted."

But in 1972 Dr. Smith was the speaker at a conference in Mount Hermon, California, where a number of nationals from *Christian Nationals* shared in the program. Paul Smith recalls, "I was amazed; and as I got to know these leaders, I was thrilled at the ways in which God was using them."

As a result Dr. Smith invited a number of nationals, including Paul Chang, to share in the great Peoples Church missions conference the following year. He likes to refer to Paul as the "million dollar man," for in response to Paul's and other nationals' testimonies the people pledged as never before. They became excited about what could be accomplished through these men and women, products of Western missionaries' efforts, now ministering in their own countries as shining lights for the gospel themselves.

The results were that he noted a strong new impetus in his congregation's commitment to missions, and he has included nationals in the conference each year since then.

Within a few years Peoples Church annual mission budget went from $600,000 to over a million dollars a year. The church began assisting 97 national leaders through *Christian Nationals;* the next year it was increased to 112, and by 1981 more than 150 *Christian Nationals* associated workers were part of the Peoples Church mission family.

Why did Paul Smith change his emphasis? He testifies that "in almost every traditional mission there had been great difficulty coming to an adequate working agreement between organizations that are primarily geared to a North American culture and great Christian leaders who have been reared in an entirely different culture. . . . We feel that they [*Christian Nationals*] treat the Christian leaders and their cultures with fairness, justice and liberality, and that they don't succumb to any of the infringing practices that have harmed the relationship between cultures in the Christian world in the past."

Since Dr. Smith wrote these gracious words, Peoples Church has added many other fine national leaders associated with other mission boards to their mission family. The mission budget rose to almost $1.5 million, and the annual missions conference has become a benchmark for church missions programs.

Few churches will be able to reach the level of involvement of Peoples Church (though many surpass her in both size and average income of membership), but every mission-minded church should set aside a portion of its mission budget for national ministries.

Gordon MacDonald, pastor and author, stated this premise in an interview for *Christian Herald,* "I think a lot of very wise congregations across the country—and denominations—are beginning to see a larger and larger percentage of their missionary giving going to organizations who can use the money wisely by exporting the money and investing it in personalities and institutions over there."[1]

It takes a special kind of love to give without strings attached—a special kind of trust to allow the Holy Spirit to direct His servants without interference or control. It takes a new kind of mission commitment to support a person they may never meet or whose work they may never see.

While this support of national Christians is on the increase, many North American churches still measure the penetration of the gospel by the number of Western missionaries there are on the field, and find it easier to raise support for couples from their own congregations than to support a national leader. Granted, a church has a responsibility to help its own members fulfill their calling, but a strong sense of responsibility to the "world family" members will bring balance to their commitments.

Today more and more churches are approaching *Christian Nationals* for advice and help about initiating an involvement with nationals, and requesting national speakers to share in their pulpit ministry.

Person to Person

Thousands of people have met, and become partners with, national Christians on a personal level after hearing them speak in mission meetings, Bible conferences, over the radio, or reading about them in mission publications.

For example, Mr. D. B. of Sumter, South Carolina, tells of how he first met the national he has been supporting for more than fifteen years. He wrote, "I was led of the Lord to support a national after receiving a challenge from Dr. Andrew Song of Hong Kong. It was a way our family could trust Him to provide for us as we became more involved in missions." He also added, "We have been blessed by the numerous nationals we've gotten to know as they came to Sumter, many visiting our home."

When Lois B. of San Jose, California, heard Gus Marwieh of Liberia speak, he said something which greatly impressed her—"No one can scratch an African where he itches like another African." As a result Lois began supporting a national worker, who today is self-supporting, and she is now involved in helping a second national.

Frequently sponsors or pastors of sponsoring churches are able to visit the national whom they are assisting and come back with enthusiastic reports.

One church, for example, sent its pastor, missions chairman, and their wives to visit a ministry in the Philippines to which they were considering giving substantial support through *Christian Nationals*. They traveled over difficult terrain and in unreliable vehicles to see one of the rural outreaches of the ministry. They talked with church planters and students in training; they met and prayed with the board, discussing in depth how best they could assist each other. As a result the church made a long range commitment both in capital funding and ongoing support, and a warm relationship has developed. They are relying on *Christian Nationals* to keep them updated on developments and to monitor this commitment.

Whether supporting a national ministry through a local church, or whether an individual or family develops a personal relationship with a national worker, certain guidelines should be observed:

1. Support the national worker through a recognized, established mission agency that will vouch for his/her doctrinal position, financial stability, and effectiveness of ministry.

2. Avoid backing a "loner"—you may find you have backed a "loser," or someone who has exploited your good will for personal gain.

3. Try to make a regular commitment. National leaders have monthly bills and family responsibility that require some kind of dependable income, just as we do. Here again there is an advantage in sending support through a responsible agency that can take up the commitment, should you have to cancel unexpectedly.

4. Many Christians in the United States may be unaware that the IRS has definite stipulations about sending funds overseas to nationals. If an individual gives a donation to a registered religious organization (i.e., church or mission), and that organization, as *part of its religious program*, supports a national worker overseas, the donation to the religious organization *is* tax deductible.

5. Write letters of encouragement, sharing your own life and prayer requests with your national worker. This "bonding" can become a source of great blessing to both parties. However, remember that many nationals cannot read and write English, and in that case the letters have to be translated—a time-consuming task. (*Christian Nationals* encourages that correspondence be done through the mission to be sure that letters are received and answered, and to avoid misunderstanding.)

6. Love gifts, of course, are appreciated, but be sure to check with the mission agency before sending gifts of money or clothing. Transfer of funds can be difficult, and duty on gifts may be very high and cause embarrassment. Frequently Western goods may not be usable in another culture.

7. Be sure to inform the mission if for some reason you can no longer continue to support the national worker. Sometimes it takes months before records reveal that regular support is not coming in; wasted time during which another sponsor could have been found.

8. Pray as regularly for your national worker as you do for

your other family members. The prayer bond between you and your worker can become a precious experience personally, and can result in his/her greater effectiveness in the ministry.

As mentioned in a previous chapter, support scales for nationals vary greatly from country to country, and from village or rural areas to cities. In some cases you may be able to take on the entire support of a national worker or a Bible school or seminary student. In others you will take a share of the support, just as you would of a Western missionary family. In addition to support, every national ministry has special projects—buildings, transportation, literature, seminars, equipment—that need funding. A sensitivity and a responsiveness to such needs can often make the difference between a national missionary just getting by and doing the task efficiently and effectively.

Mission agencies will have evaluated the needs for these projects and the availability of local resources before attempting to raise funds for them elsewhere. It is wise to follow their lead. *Christian Nationals* insists that the local board approve any project, whether for the ministry or personal needs of the workers, to avoid the human temptation for recipients to take advantage of donors.

Every mission agency assisting nationals has its own basis for support. *Christian Nationals* suggests at least twenty-five dollars per month for a worker and twenty dollars per month for a Bible school student, since the costs of handling and/or transferring funds and communicating with nationals has increased greatly in recent years. The average support is usually in the neighborhood of one hundred dollars per month.

If you do not have a preference, a worker will be selected from the country of your choice, if so desired. Once you have agreed to assist a national for a certain monthly amount, you will receive his or her picture (or a family photo) and testimony, plus three field reports or letters a year.

As of this writing, *Christian Nationals* is assisting some 1,500 workers and Bible school students in almost forty countries involved in ministries of evangelism, church planting, education, youth work, child care, and development and relief.

Can We Do More?

Most people interested enough in missions to read a book about it are already heavily committed to various programs to which they have been drawn by the Holy Spirit. The natural question is, "But I'm already deeply involved. How can I do more?"

A closer look at our resources would probably indicate that it *is* possible to do more. We live in a world of economic pressures and the subtle "seduction of riches," and we are surrounded by a narcissistic society which says "me first." Almost without knowing it many of our wants and desires have been interpreted as "needs."

In 1980 a survey of over six hundred business managers in the United States and several other Western countries included the following multiple choice question:[2]

Most people naturally tend to be more concerned with:
   a. the desire to help others
   b. their own needs and desires
   c. a combination of both

A majority (seventy-seven percent) checked "b"—in direct opposition to the biblical instruction, "Do nothing out of selfish ambition or vain conceit, but in humility consider others better than yourselves" (Phil. 2:3).

There are overwhelming needs in the world:

Sixteen million refugees and displaced people live in desolation or wander without hope in this world, according to World Relief.

Starvation kills fifty thousand people every day, and one billion (four times the population of the United States) are hungry (UN Development Program).

More than one quarter of all the people on the earth exist on incomes of less than three dollars a week. The economic imbalance becomes uncomfortable when one compares the per capita gross national product of some Third World countries with that of the United States:

GNP PER CAPITA[3]

North America	$12,405
Latin America	2,063
Africa	783
South Asia (includes India, Bangladesh, and Pakistan)	251

It is difficult to plead ignorance to such needs, for we are bombarded by our newspapers and T.V.—yet many of us are jaded by anguish, and remain untouched by pain in the midst of our affluence.

Dr. Paul Brand, former missionary doctor in India, reiterated this dichotomy as he observed it when coming home on furlough:

In India we treated leprosy patients for $3 per year. . . . Yet we turned many away for lack of funds. Then we came to America where churches were heatedly discussing their million-dollar gymnasiums and the cost of landscaping, or a new steeple (together) with sponsoring seminars on tax shelters for members to conserve their accumulated wealth. . . . I could not force a telling image from my mind of the Madras woman slowly starving to death while her lipoma tumor grew and grew . . . remember the body will have health only if each cell regards the needs of the whole body.[4]

Frank Gaebelein put it this way:

Never have I heard at a Bible conference a responsible treat-ment of Amos' strong words about the injustices done through the misuse of wealth—nothing about the major witness of the prophets against the idolatry of things and the oppression that may be entailed in accumulating them.[5]

Christ in His compassion would not have us forget that people die of starvation every day. One quarter of the world's population suffers grinding poverty while another quarter revels in unparalleled prosperity.

Graffiti seen on a Jamaican building sounds the warning we all must hear: "The poor can't take it no more."

The key to equality and justice lies within the body itself. The strength, energy and sustenance available to the body must be distributed to all parts, to every member, to all joints, so that its potential for work, production, and excel-lence in performing its assigned task may be fulfilled.

The early church recognized this key. Believers in Jerusalem sold their possessions and shared them with other believers. As a result, "There were no needy persons among them" (Acts: 4:34). The "family tie" was very strong.

Paul, on the other hand, had to rebuke the Corinthians for eating and drinking too much while their poor brothers and sisters were left hungry. Paul scathingly asked, ". . . do you . . . humiliate those who have nothing?" (1 Corin-thians 11:22).

In another letter he urged them to give out of their abundance that "there might be equality." Paul did this graciously, acknowledging their love for Christ, yet remind-ing them that Christ, who had every right and possibility for riches, became poor for their sakes so that they might be enriched.

The resulting outpouring of generosity for the poor in Jerusalem was a beautiful demonstration of cross-cultural concern in Christ.

The history of missions is incomplete without the stories of faithfulness and sacrifice of thousands upon thousands of Christians who have "held the ropes" in partnership with those on the "front lines."

In his book *Nothing to Win but the World* Clay Cooper tells about a young man and his wife who were accepted for missionary service, but because of poor health had to turn around and go back home. Consequently they determined to make all the money they could to extend the kingdom of God.

The young man's father was a dentist who made unfermented communion wine as a sideline. The couple took over his "hobby" and fulfilled their dream of world mission in a unique way. They built it up into a multi-million dollar business and contributed hundreds of thousands of dollars to missions. The grape juice still carries the family name—Welch.

Most sensitive and mature Christians are aware of the need to do something about the poverty stricken—in body and soul. Many feel helpless in the face of graft, greed, corruption, big business, sheer numbers, anonymity and geographical distance. As a result, it's easier to do nothing.

Even the International Consultation on Simple Lifestyle, held in London in 1980, left this question hanging, "How will simplifying your lifestyle help the poorest of the poor?"

Recognizing that multi-national business and political powers and graft often make it difficult to change the hopeless plight of millions who live in abject poverty, nevertheless the consultation vowed:

We intend to re-examine our income and expenditure in order to manage on less and give away more.

If this is to be more than eccentricity or personal piety, there must be a way to channel the overflow to those in need. Many give generously in the West today; in America almost $20 billion was given to churches and religious organizations in 1979.[6] But it is estimated that ninety-six percent of *all money given for religious causes is spent on the six percent of the world's population that speaks English.* In other words, only four percent of our tithes and offerings go to help our brothers and sisters who live as part of the ninety-four percent of the world's population.

As a result, a husband and wife medical team in India had to visit surrounding villages without medical care, riding on a dilapidated old scooter, carrying all the medicine they had in a black bag on the wife's lap. Up until a few years ago they supported themselves by opening an office for "paying" patients (one or two dollars per visit) in the evenings after returning from the villages.

. . . And pastors in Jamaica have to give up a full-time ministry in order to take a job so they can feed their families.

. . . Or thousands of children in the never-before-reached Chittagong Hills area of Bangladesh have *never* gone to school—and will not be able to do so until funds can be found to pay teachers at fifty-five dollars a month.

. . . And workers in Ghana have had to restrict the highly effective discipleship program of New Life For All to within a short radius of Kumasi, because they can't buy the gas to take them out to the more needy areas.

. . . Or . . .

There are probably very few reading this book who could not cut twenty-five dollars worth of "fat" out of his or her monthly budget—yet that would enable a student to attend Bible school in many Third World countries; or would pay half a month's salary for an evangelist to work in a Hindu village; or almost half of a Christian teacher's salary in Bangladesh.

Most of us could cut out a lot more "fat" than that. And when it comes to Christian ministries, there is no lack of legitimate, credible, trustworthy organizations who would transfer our resources efficiently.

Ronald Sider has raised a clarion call for involvement:

> The Church of Jesus Christ is the most universal body in the world today. All we need to do is truly obey the One we rightly worship. To obey will mean to follow. And He lives among the poor and oppressed, seeking justice for those in agony. In our time, following in His steps will mean simple, personal lifestyles. It will mean transformed churches with a corporate lifestyle consistent with worship of the God of the poor. It will mean costly commitment to structural change. Do Christians today have that kind of faith and courage?[7]

Assisting Nationals by Going

John Kyle, director of missions for Inter-Varsity Christian Fellowship and prime mover behind Urbana '81, feels strongly that young people going overseas for a short term ought to have their first cross-cultural experience working for or with a national leader.

A few years ago this would have been an impossible dream, but as we have seen, the church in the Third World today has a great corps of dedicated, effective leaders, and many would welcome assistance, either short or longer term, from *skilled* Western Christian workers.

Some mission organizations provide such opportunities, though generally they send short termers to work with Western missionaries. Missions such as the Africa Inland Mission and the Sudan Interior Mission assign their missionaries to work under the church, and could possibly arrange for a short termer to do the same.

Some missions lend their personnel to work for an independent national ministry. For example, the OMF has for many years provided missionary staff to teach at the prestigious Singapore Bible College, one of the most highly acclaimed Bible schools in the Orient.

At the request of Dr. Chris Marantika, principal of the Evangelical Theological Seminary of Indonesia, O.C. Ministries lent two couples. The fact that these missionaries are working *for* a national organization has made it less likely they will have to leave under Indonesia's growing legislation against foreign mission work.

As a mission dedicated primarily to working *with* independent national ministries, Latin American Mission (LAM) is unique in the field. Each autonomous ministry that has been established by LAM is governed by a national board, and LAM provides American personnel at the request of the national board. Each missionary signs a three or four year contract with the ministry, which is reviewed at the end of that period.

LAM promotes the financial needs of the various autonomous organizations as needs arise, though they do not support individual nationals as such. The restructuring has not been without its trauma (see p. 156), but basically mission and national leaders are happy with the outcome. One LAM official said, "They've done a lot of fabulous things which would never have been done under the old structure."

Whether a person serves as a career missionary or a short termer under national leadership, he or she ought to have special training in cross-cultural communications. Working in another culture is, at best, fraught with frustrations, but serving under a national board will require adaptations of attitude and lifestyle, if it is to be a mutually beneficial experience.

Some basic guidelines for working for a national ministry are:

1. *Be ready for culture shock.* What may seem cute, exciting, and wonderful the first few days will soon be frustrating, strange, and wrong, unless you are prepared for cultural differences.

For example, a church was sending a group of its young people to various overseas countries for summer ministry. The leader had arranged for them to go in couples (boy and girl, though not married) thinking this would be safer.

The young people were surprised to learn that young men and women are discouraged from being seen together in public or going anywhere privately in a number of Third World cultures, and that unless they are very careful, they would be looked upon as immoral. They had not realized that what seemed wise from their point of view could be seriously misconstrued in another culture, and thus hinder their effectiveness.

2. *Go with a servant attitude.* Be ready to do whatever you are asked; don't feel you know it all or give the impression that "back home we do it better."

Many groups go to Mexico from North America because of its proximity. But a Bible school leader in Mexico shared that these groups often leave the impression that sight-seeing and having a good time were more important than serving. They are still talking about the group, however, that went to paint dormitories and clean and renovate washrooms during the students' holidays, and who worked so long and hard they hardly left the campus the whole time they were there.

3. *Try to develop a warm, intimate relationship with at least one national.* This may be difficult to do on a short-term assignment, especially where language is a problem, but it is the only way you are going to get an "in" to the culture and the hearts of the people. Don't be afraid to say, "I want to learn; tell me what I'm doing wrong; correct me if I make a blunder."

It is unfortunate that occasionally a Westerner may make it difficult to become intimate with a national. One short termer in Africa said she was reprimanded by the staff of the girls' school where she had come to teach because she "hung around" with the girls and spent her days off doing things with them.

On the other hand, the short termer may be tempted to spend all his/her time with the Western missionaries since that is more familiar and comfortable. Nationals, generally, will not seek out the foreigner's friendship, not wanting to impose themselves on the Westerner. But once they see that you genuinely want to break the barriers, open your heart, and share in their lives, the relationship can become one of the most precious in your life—and you will have gained a true brother or sister in Christ.

Whether you are privileged to go and become personally involved in a national ministry, or whether you are asked to sacrifice your resources to enable a national to fulfill his calling, you are strengthening your "family ties"—and the benefits will more than outweigh the cost.

Notes

1. Gordon MacDonald, "Your Church in God's Global Plan," *Christian Herald*, November, 1980, p. 52.
2. Jeanne Polston Greene, "People Management: New Directions for the '80s," *Administrative Management*, January, 1981, p. 25.
3. 1983 World Population Data Sheet, Population Reference Bureau, 1337 Connecticut Avenue, N.W., Washington, D.C.
4. Paul Brand, "Fat Cells in the Body: Issues of Loyalty," *Christianity Today*, October 10, 1980, p. 45.
5. Frank E. Gaebelein, "Challenging Christians to the Simple Life," *Christianity Today*, September 21, 1979, pp. 23, 24.
6. American Association of Fund Raising.
7. Ronald J. Sider, *Rich Christians in an Age of Hunger*, A *Biblical Study*, Inter-Varsity Press, Downers Grove, 1977, p. 225.

12

WHAT OUR INVOLVEMENT IN NATIONAL MINISTRIES CAN MEAN TO US

There can be no greater satisfaction for a Christian than to know that he or she is walking in obedience to God, fully yielded to His revealed will.

This is the most meaningful and satisfying result of our involvement in national ministries; for we have seen throughout the pages of this book that partnership with others in the family of God is His design.

When Paul urged the Corinthians to take part in the relief of the saints, He elaborated the benefits, warning, however, that if they sowed sparingly they would reap accordingly. But look at the bountiful rewards for those who give generously for needs of the family of God:

abundant blessing;

enough of everything so that we can give even more;

the supply and multiplication of our resources;

the needs of God's people met;

thanksgiving poured out to God because of our gifts;

God glorified as others see the results of the gifts;

those receiving the gifts will feel drawn to us in a new and deeper relationship;

the rest of the family will pray for us (2 Cor. 9:14-15).

How does God fulfill these promises when we support a national across the world in another culture, whose language we cannot speak and whom we may never meet?

The following excerpts from correspondence between a

school teacher in the United States and a Korean church planter speak for themselves. The letters were translated from Korean by another Korean pastor whose use of English may not be perfect, but is beautifully graphic.

Dear Sponsor,
   I received the Christmas present thankfully. With the gift I treated the old men with rice-bread and soup. Our church was filled with thanks and the old men were thankful. . . .

Yong-Tae

An explanatory letter by the Korean supervisor of the church planters gives a little more insight into Yong-Tae's situation:

We visited Yong-Tae and his lovely wife in a very remote mountain valley where they have moved to serve the Lord . . . the church building is completed, but you can see by the picture that the manse they are living in has a lot of work to be done on it . . . there are about thirty adults coming out for services . . . until the church was started three years ago there were no Christians and no knowledge of the gospel.

Yong-Tae's sponsor replied, sending her picture and telling something about herself, ending her letter,

Just four years ago I learned what it really meant to know Christ as my personal Lord and Savior. Since then being a Christian has been an exciting experience. . . . I will be praying for you regularly and your wife. I pray too for Mr. Kim and his bride [about whom Yong-Tae had written] that Christ would bless their marriage. Please pray for me that I may love God with all my heart and soul and mind.

Joanne

Some time later Joanne sent a gift so that windows could be put into the uncompleted manse, and Yong-Tae responded:

Thank you for your letters and the gift. It was the first letter from a foreign country. . . . When I looked on your picture my tears flew. I met you in our Lord's love and thank the Lord who introduced you to me. I could repair the house with your help.

I wish to invite you when we finish the remending of the house. All my church members saw your pictures and letters and were glad and had thanks. The non-Christians had the same impression when they see them. . . . I pray to the Lord and hope you will be a powerful servant of the Lord.

And a few months later Joanne wrote again:

How happy I was to receive your wonderful letter and to know that you received the money and will be able to finish the house. I am thankful that our relationship to one another in Christ is a witness to non-Christians of how Christ binds us together in love, no matter where we are in the world.

After telling of her recent vacation and her plans for the new school year [she has been a teacher for seventeen years] she added,

I would ask you to pray too that I can spend less money so that I can give more to the Lord's work around the world.

This kind of sensitivity to personal lifestyle is just one more benefit of becoming involved with a national worker. It is difficult to continue indulging ourselves with luxuries when we have a close relationship with a dedicated Christian who cannot have the essentials.

It was important to Joanne, a single school teacher, to find ways to cut back in her lifestyle so that Yong-Tae could have windows in his house before winter set in in Korea.

The supporters of the Giriama workers in Africa learned that for a mere one hundred dollars they could provide a water tank to collect rain water running off the corrugated iron roof, thus saving a two-mile daily hike to the nearest river during the dry season. They were glad for the opportunity to deny themselves so their workers could have water.

Lifestyle becomes more than a controversial theory when we have real live "family members" whose own poverty could be alleviated if we cut back "the fat" in our affluence. As one sponsor wrote, "Investing in people is so much more fascinating than investing in oil, utilities, or real estate."

Lifestyle refers not only to controlling and prioritizing the use of our material possessions, but our time. Our values are revealed by the way we spend our time, whether it be putting in overtime at the office, socializing, developing relationships, or cleaning house. The Korean church has demonstrated the high priority it places on time spent in prayer. Ever since the Korean war, churches have opened their doors for prayer meetings, and the countryside reverberates with the ringing of the churchbells calling people to assemble for prayer early every day of the week. There is no question that there is a strong correlation between this extraordinary prayer and the phenomenal growth of the church in recent years.

Thus when Yong-Tae writes his sponsor, Joanne, that the Christians are praying for her every day, she knows these are not idle platitudes.

Not everyone who supports a national will receive detailed personalized letters from his/her worker; many of them, like many of us, find it hard to express themselves on paper. And some from their cultural background find it too difficult to write about their "success" (so expected in the West) lest it seem boastful.

But once we begin supporting and praying for a national ministry, our horizons broaden. Political and military crises become points for urgent prayer. We begin to read with our antennae raised to pick up information about the areas with which we are involved.

This is what happens when we strengthen the family ties between ourselves and the rest of God's world-family. Every shift in policy in government, and every disaster is evaluated as to how it will affect a family member. You know the feeling when someone you love is on vacation and you hear of a tornado or flood in the area. Even the national weather report gets special attention for the places where family members are living; and if unusual events are reported, we get on the phone immediately to find out if everything is all right.

Just so, our involvement with national ministries makes us sensitive to events in their part of the world, and we want to learn everything we can about the country and its people.

What a wonderful way to train children to be "world Christians" too. Many families sponsor children in the Third World, not only because the youngsters need help, but to help their own children begin to pray and take an interest in their "brother or sister" across the sea.

An added blessing comes when the national worker can visit the home of sponsors. Of course, these opportunities are limited because many cannot speak English well enough to do deputation in the West. But those who do come try to visit their own sponsors if at all possible, and it can be a unique experience for all concerned.

Sometimes it is humorous when two cultures cross for the first time. One national on his first trip from Zambia, where he deals constantly with the powers of evil spirits and demon worship, received quite a shock when he went to his room in the home of an American pastor. As he knelt down beside the bed to pray, the whole bed began to heave and roll as though possessed by spirits. Terrified, he rushed downstairs to tell the pastor, who controlled his mirth as he introduced him to the mysteries of the waterbed!

Conversely, the nationals can add so much to our lives

when they stay in our homes. One young Christian family invited a Nigerian to stay with them while he was in their area. The young couple had only recently come to the Lord, and had never had family devotions with their children. As they asked David about his home and family, he told them about how he read the Bible and prayed with his children every day. The couple asked if he would lead devotions in their home and show them how it could be done. That family will never forget the lessons they learned from their Nigerian brother.

On a broader scale churches are finding that adding nationals to their mission family brings a new dimension to missions. Peoples Church in Toronto, though a leader in church missions programs, is only one among many churches whose mission budget expanded tremendously as the church people met nationals and realized the potentia[l] in these gifted servants of God.

Your church does not have to be large and affluent to make a meaningful contribution to a national. Some years ago a small independent church on the east coast of the United States pledged fifty dollars per month—the full support of a young Malaysian evangelist. He planted a church in Johore Bahru, which in a few years grew to a membership larger than theirs. You can imagine what a thrill this has been to be able to reproduce themselves in Muslim Malaysia. Meanwhile the Christians in Malaysia caught the spirit of its supporting United States church, and now help a number of missionaries in other parts of the world. In 1980 its mission budget reached thirty-three thousand dollars, and it has planted six daughter churches in other areas.

Nationals ministering in our churches can bring a new dimension to our service. For example, when the Mizo choir traveled in North America for three months under sponsorship of *Christian Nationals,* thousands of Christians saw a new kind of missionary commitment. The young Mizos, from the Indian state of Mizoram, sandwiched between Bangladesh and Burma, come from a tribe that had been headhunters just eighty-five years ago. With the coming of the gospel, a great revival spread through the tribe, and today ninety-five percent of the people in this land-locked, poverty-sticken state are Christians.

To the Mizos missions is their message; missions is their way of life; and their "Samaria" is the rest of the land of India with its 650 million people. In 1978 this tribe of a quarter million people had almost 150 missionaries in surrounding Indian states, all supported by the sacrificial giving of these subsistence farmers. The choir members told of ingenious ways they used to raise funds for missions: for example, families set aside one stick of wood a day from their firewood to be collected by the church at the end of the month and sold in town for missions.

The women have devised another method of raising mission funds. When they cook rice, they measure out what is needed for the family and then take back one handful, which is placed in a special container. At the end of the month this rice is taken to the church, where it is sold for missions. This amount is hardly noticed by the family, they say, but when it is done twice a day by every Christian family for a whole year the total amount can be considerable.[1]

Funds raised in this way may seem insignificant to meet our accelerating mission expenditures, but the zeal and dedication must be unmatched anywhere. No wonder people's hearts were touched by the ministry of the Mizos. The response of this pastor is indicative of their impact:

Thank you so much for allowing us the privilege of being ministered to by these fantastic, committed Christians from Mizoram. We so much appreciated their concert here, and I can personally testify that the choir has had a profound influence on the lives of many of our people.

It would be unrealistic to assume that national Christians are more spiritual, more mature, and more dedicated than our brothers and sisters right around us. But on the other hand, many have suffered more, endured greater persecution and harrassment, faced ostracism and hostilities from family members, stood up to fanatical religious powers— and through these experiences have developed insights and strengths they can share with us.

Gordon MacDonald believes some of the greatest preaching today is being done by leaders from Latin America, Africa, and Asia, who have gone through the testings that may yet be ahead of us. He affirms:

Our Third-World brothers and sisters know what it's like to really pursue the spirit of wisdom because they have nothing else to survive on. They know what it's like to be hungry, they know what it's like to be homeless. They have a perspective on the Gospel and what it means to live the Gospel with reality. I look forward in the coming years to the perspective we're going to receive from the Third-World church as it returns to minister to the North American churches.[2]

In a day when the breakup of the family is of deep concern to us all, the church is going to extraordinary efforts to heal the shattered and bruised lives of people whose personal worlds are falling apart. We may be tempted to look inward and to concentrate on the problems closer to home. But it is by an increased awareness of God's sovereign purpose in this troubled world that life as it is makes sense. He has promised, "I will build My Church," and He is doing it. It is His first priority, and if we walk in obedience to Him, it must be ours. To be an involved, concerned member of

God's "world family" takes a special effort of the mind and heart and an openness to the wooing of the Holy Spirit who wants to use us to heal the.hurts and help remedy the inequities in the larger "family."

As fellow heirs with Christ the "inheritance" is available to all who trust Him. Yet millions have never heard that our Elder Brother died for them, and that they can also have a part in that great inheritance of love. As privileged members of God's world family, we have been called upon to share our resources with them, so that the world might yet say, "See how these brothers [and sisters] love each other."

Notes

1. Lorry Lutz, *The Mizos: God's Hidden People*, Christian Nationals Evangelism Commission, San Jose, California, 1980, p. 36.
2. Gordon MacDonald, "Your Church in God's Global Plan," *Christian Herald*, November, 1980, p. 49.

APPENDIX A

Excerpts from a paper delivered by Allen B. Finley at the EFMA/IFMA Retreat 1977, and later given as a workshop at the National Conference of the Association of Church Missions Committees.

Guidelines for Selection
of National Ministries

1. Determine and study priorities in the area where the ministry is developing.
2. Study the history and development of the ministry itself. It has generally proven best to aid strategic aspects of an existing ministry rather than to try to finance someone's "vision." There are, however, exceptions where outside assistance is needed to launch some new strategic ministry. This requires careful analysis.
3. Inquire diligently into its doctrinal stand. Question both those who lead the ministry and others who know them and their testimonies.
4. Study the relationships of the ministry to the national church with which it is associated. Determine if there are tensions or if the leaders are under discipline.
5. Study its relationships with other national church bodies or movements.
6. Determine its attitude toward evangelical fellowships.
7. Study its membership and relationships to various na-

tional and international councils and/or fellowships, including the WCC.

8. Ask other Christians in the area their opinion of its relationship to the government, and its legal standing and property ownership, if any.

9. Determine if it has local financial support and backing.

10. Analyze the basic objectives of the ministry, including its immediate and long-range goals.

11. Gain the opinions and evaluations of Christian leaders, missionaries, and mission agencies that are familiar with work and needs in the area in which the ministry is to serve.

12. Study its administrative structure. Give special attention to the governing board and determine accountability.

13. Discuss frankly the ministry's financial policies and its willingness to follow the scriptural basis set forth in 2 Corinthians 8:21 KJV: "Providing things honest in the sight of God and all men that the ministry be not blamed."

14. To avoid confusion and credibility gaps, determine if the ministry has already directed appeals to individuals and agencies abroad.

APPENDIX B

Principles For Reciprocal Commitment
Between Christian Nationals
And Indigenous Movements

Prepared By: Allen B. Finley, International President

The Principles of this commitment are as follows:

1. There shall be agreement on basic Bible doctrines adhered to by *Christian Nationals* and the indigenous ministries.

2. *Christian Nationals* is committed to pursue energetically a policy of non-exploitation of nationals and indigenous ministries. The transferring of funds which God's people feel prompted by the Holy Spirit to share is done with utmost care, and these funds go as designated.

3. *Christian Nationals* does not interfere with the administration of indigenous programs. Neither does *Christian Nationals* send funds to any national working alone or independently. All must be under the overseership of a recognized national body or board. A working agreement mutually acceptable shall be drawn up between *Christian Nationals* and each field board.

4. The boards (organizations) which God has led into fellowship with *Christian Nationals* agree to maintain their indigenous nature and to strive for full self-support.

5. The leaders of indigenous programs assisted by *Christian Nationals* agree to limit any appeal for funds outside of their own nation or area to that which is carried out in full cooperation with *Christian Nationals*. All mailings of personal letters or publications from the national organization or individuals related to the organization, for the purpose of raising support, must be done through the *Christian Nationals* international offices.

6. Indigenous programs agree not to obligate *Christian Nationals* for any project they wish to develop without prior agreement with *Christian Nationals* in writing in advance. That enables *Christian Nationals* to prayerfully consider its faith commitments.

7. All speakers who go abroad to promote these projects shall go in full agreement with and under the established deputation program of *Christian Nationals*. All funds raised shall be channeled through *Christian Nationals* for those projects or areas so represented.

8. The indigenous programs agree to permit *Christian Nationals* to publicize their work. They will provide photos and testimonies of workers so that *Christian Nationals* can gain interest and support. Further, all workers receiving assistance through *Christian Nationals* shall write and deliver through field offices the required letters and reports. These letters and reports may be edited to conform to mailing procedure limitations and in consideration of *Christian Nationals'* policies.

9. *Christian Nationals* agrees to give full explanation of its relationships with other missions in any publicity so as not to confuse God's people with unclear reporting, nor to discredit or violate the indigenous nature of the work.

10. The indigenous group agrees to publish its audited financial report annually and to send a copy to *Christian*

Nationals' international president, and to permit him, or his appointee, to visit them at any time.

11. While *Christian Nationals* does not interfere with the administration of indigenous projects, it does seek to contribute to their effectiveness by sharing ideas, providing some appropriate literature and tapes, helping certain workers attend seminars, etc. National works and/or workers assisted by *Christian Nationals* will cooperate in this effort by promptly filling out and returning questionnaires and evaluation forms occasionally requested by the international headquarters. Workers will also report special blessings and successes which may be of help to other workers.

Written: 1968
Revised: 1974
Revised: 1978
Revised: 1983

BIBLIOGRAPHY

1. Books

Allen, Roland, *The Spontaneous Expansion of the Church*, World Dominion Press, London, 1946.

Berney, James, Editor, *You Can Tell the World, A Mission Reader*, Inter-Varsity Press, Downers Grove, 1979.

Camara, D. H., *Revolution Through Peace*, Harper & Row, New York, 1971.

Cervin, Russell A., *Mission in Ferment*, Covenant Press, Chicago, 1977.

Clark, Dennis E., *The Third World and Mission*, Word Books, Waco, 1971.

Coggins, Wade T. and E. L. Frizen, Jr., *Evangelical Missions Tomorrow*, William Carey Library, Pasadena, 1977.

Cook, Harold R., *Highlights of Christian Missions*, Moody Press, Chicago, 1967.

Cooper, Clay, *Nothing to Win but the World*, Zondervan Publishing House, Grand Rapids, 1965.

Costas, Orlando E., *The Church and Its Mission, A Shattering Critique from the Third World*, Tyndale Publishers, Wheaton, 1974.

Cowen, Paul A., *China and Christianity*, Harvard, Cambridge, 1963.

Dayton, Edward R. and David A. Fraiser, *Planning Strategy for World Evangelization*, Eerdmans Publishing Company, Grand Rapids, 1980.

Douglas, J. D., *Let the Earth Hear His Voice*, Worldwide Publications, Minneapolis, 1975.

Engstrom, Ted, *What in the World is God Doing? The New Face of Missions*, Word Publishers, Waco, 1978.

Fenton, Horace, *Myths about Missions*, Inter-Varsity Press, Downers Grove, 1973.

Fife, Eric S. and Arthur S. Glasser, *Missions in Crisis*, Inter-Varsity Press, Downers Grove, 1961.

Fuller, Harold, *Mission Church Dynamics*, William Carey Library, Pasadena, 1980.

Getz, Gene A., *The Measure of A Church*, Regal G/L, Glendale, 1975.

Kane, Herbert, *A Global View of Christian Missions*, Baker Book House, Grand Rapids, 1971.

Keyes, Lawrence, *The Last Age of Missions*, William Carey Library, Pasadena, 1983.

Kraft, C. H. and Tom N. Wisley, *Readings in Dynamic Indigeneity*, William Carey Library, Pasadena, 1979.

Latourette, Kenneth Scott, *Missions Tomorrow*, Harper and Brothers, New York, 1936.

Latourette, Kenneth Scott, *Christianity in a Revolutionary Age*, Harper & Row, New York, Vol. 5, 1962.

Lindsell, Harold, *The Church's Worldwide Mission*, Word Books, Waco, 1966.

Lutz, Lorry, *Born to Lose, Bound to Win*, Harvest House, Irvine, 1980.

McGavran, Donald, *Understanding Church Growth*, Eerdmans Publishing Company, Grand Rapids, 1970.

Miura, Ayako, *The Wind is Howling*, Inter-Varsity Press, Downers Grove, 1977.

Neill, Stephen, *A History of Christian Missions*, Penguin Books, Baltimore, 1964.

Nelson, Marlin L., *The How and Why of Third World Missions*, William Carey Library, Pasadena, 1976.

Peters, George W., *A Biblical Theology of Missions*, Moody Press, Chicago, 1972.

Pollock, John C., *A Foreign Devil in China*, Worldwide Publications, Minneapolis, 1971.

Sider, Ronald J., *Rich Christians in an Age of Hunger: A Biblical Study*, Inter-Varsity Press, Downers Grove, 1977.

Soltau, Stanley, *Missions at the Crossroads*, Van Kampen Press, Wheaton, 1954.

Tegenfeldt, Herman, *A Century of Growth, The Kachin Baptist Church of Burma*, William Carey Library, Pasadena, 1974.

Wagner, C. Peter, *Church/Mission Tensions Today*, Moody Press, Chicago, 1972.

Wagner, C. Peter and Edward R. Dayton, *Unreached Peoples '81*, David C. Cook Publishing Co., Elgin, 1981.

Wilson, Samuel, editor, *12th Edition Mission Handbook*, Missions Advanced Research and Communication Center, Monrovia, 1979.

Winter, Ralph, *The 25 Unbelievable Years 1945-1969*, William Carey Library, Pasadena, 1969.

2. Periodicals

Brand, Paul, "Fat Cells in the Body: Issues of Loyalty," *Christianity Today*, October 10, 1980.

Conn, Harvie, "The Money Barrier Between Sending and Receiving Churches," *Evangelical Missions Quarterly*, Vol. 14, No. 14, October 1978.

Coon, Roger E., "Unchanging Task: Changing Roles," *Evangelical Missions Quarterly*, Vol. 16, No. 4, October 1980.

"COWE: 200,000 by the Year 2000," (editorial), *Christianity Today*, August 8, 1980.

Donald, Kenneth, "What is Wrong With Foreign Money for National Pastors?" *Evangelical Missions Quarterly*, Vol. 13, No. 1, January 1977.

EMISsary, Evangelical Missions Information Service, Vol. 11, No. 3, June 1980.

Fuller, Harold, "Guiding Principles in Mission-Church Relationships," *Africa Pulse*, Evangelical Missions Information Service, Vol. 13, No. 3, November 1980.

Gaebelein, Frank E., "Challenging Christians to the Simple Life," *Christianity Today*, October 10, 1980.

Greene, Jeanne Polston, "People Management: New Directions for the '80s," *Administrative Management*, January 1981.

Keidel, Levi O., "The Peril of Giving," *World Vision*, November 1971.

Kenyon, John, "Your Church in God's Global Plan," *Christian Herald*, November 1980.

Lamb, David, "Spreading African Christianity," *Los Angeles Times*, March 21, 1980.

Lovering, Kerry E., "The Ethnic Approach: One Tribe at a Time," *Africa Now*, No. 88, September/October 1976.

Lutz, Lorry, "Mission Money Isn't Just for Westerners Any More," *Christian Life*, May 1971.

MacDonald, Gordon, "Your Church in God's Plan," *Christian Herald*, November 1980.

McQuicken, J. R., "The Thailand Consultation by B. Hogard," *Mission Frontiers*, Vol. 2, No. 8, August 1980.

Neill, Stephen, "Building the Church on Two Continents," *Christianity Today*, July 18, 1980.

Palms, Roger C., "Three Billion People: How Shall They Hear?" *World Evangelization*, Bulletin No. 20, September 1980.

Plueddeman, James E., "Church Maturity: Old Hat?" *Evangelical Missions Quarterly*, Vol. 16, No. 3, July 1980.

Pretiz, Paul E., "Church-Mission Tensions Today," *Latin America Evangelist*, March/April 1980.

"Reflections on '71," *Evangelical Missions Quarterly*, Summer, 1972.

Richard, D. John, "Evangelical Cooperation," *AIM*, November 1980.

Strom, Donna, "Christianity and Culture Change Among the Mizo," *Missiology*, Vol. VIII, No. 3, July 1980.

The Thailand Statement, "Thailand 80," *World Evangelization*, September 1980.

A Learning Guide for a six week group study on the principles of this book is available for a nominal fee from:

Christian Nationals Evangelism Commission

1470 North Fourth Street, P.O. Box 15025

San Jose, CA 95115-0025
or
P.O. Box 215,
Islington, Ontario M9A 4X2